The Resilient School Library

The Resilient School Library

Carol A. Doll and Beth Doll

LIBRARIES UNLIMITED

AN IMPRINT OF ABC-CLIO, LLC
Santa Barbara, California • Denver, Colorado • Oxford, England

Library of Congress Cataloging-in-Publication Data

Doll, Carol Ann, 1949–
   The resilient school library / Carol A. Doll and Beth Doll.
       p. cm.
   Includes bibliographical references and index.
   ISBN 978-1-59158-639-5 (acid-free paper)   1. School libraries—United States.
2. School libraries—Evaluation.   3. Resilience (Personality trait) in children.
4. Academic achievement—Psychological aspects.   I. Doll, Beth.   II. Title.
   Z675.S3D5995   2010
   027.8—dc22   2010021570

ISBN: 978-1-59158-639-5

14   13   12   11   10   1   2   3   4   5

This book is also available on the World Wide Web as an eBook.
Visit www.abc-clio.com for details.

Libraries Unlimited
An Imprint of ABC-CLIO, LLC

ABC-CLIO, LLC
130 Cremona Drive, P.O. Box 1911
Santa Barbara, California 93116-1911

This book is printed on acid-free paper ∞
Manufactured in the United States of America

We lovingly dedicate this book to our father,
also a university professor and author.

Contents

1   Introduction to Resilient School Libraries 1

2   Evaluating the Effectiveness of Resilience Plans 7

3   Academic Efficacy 23

4   Self-Selected Learning Goals 37

5   Behavioral Self-Control 47

6   Caring and Authentic Relationships Between Teachers and Students 63

7   The Role of Peer Relationships in Resilience 77

8   The Role of Family in Resilience 91

9   Pedagogical Techniques to Support Resilience 101

Appendices

     A. Template for Planning for Resilience 109

     B. Resilience and *Standards for the 21st-Century Learner* 111

     C. ClassMaps Survey 2007 for School Libraries 115

Index 119

1

Introduction to Resilient School Libraries

Children and teens are today's hope for tomorrow, and growing up is difficult in the best of conditions. In tough conditions, it is much more difficult for children to grow into competent and well-adjusted adults. Still, some children do succeed despite childhood hardships, and these are the *resilient* children. *Resilience* is the capacity of children to grow up to be successful, content, and competent even though they are faced with adversities like poverty, violence, illness, or neglect (Doll, Zucker, & Brehm, 2004; Werner, 2006). Recent research suggests that the most important things to foster children's resilience are environments that give them the support and skills they need. Specific types of environmental support and skills are necessary to help youth overcome adversity and thrive. Descriptions of these environments, and the strategies to create them, are central topics of this book.

WHAT IS RESILIENCE?

A remarkable series of research studies describing children's development was begun in the 1960s and 1970s (Werner, 2006). Researchers were trying to understand why some children grew into competent and successful adults while other children from the same neighborhoods did not. They began to carefully follow groups of children from the time of their birth until they were adolescents or even young adults. Meticulous records were kept of risk factors that might be present in the children's families, such as poverty, parental health problems, parental unemployment, low parent education, or marital discord. Other records described the children's communities and included information on community violence and crime rates, or poor schools. Still other records described the children themselves—their intelligence, sociability, physical activity levels, or personal health. Some of the studies used these factors to predict which children would later fail in school, while other studies tried to predict other important outcomes, such as adult criminal activity, unemployment, mental illness, or dishonorable discharge from the military. Even though there were several different studies conducted in the United States, Great Britain, Australia, and other countries, the results were surprisingly similar. Only 8 or 10 factors actually predicted the children's success or failure, and these were the same factors in each of the independent studies.

(Table 1.1 describes these factors and the outcomes that they predicted.) Interestingly, most of the important factors listed in Table 1.1 are characteristics of the children's families and communities—and not of the children themselves. These results show how important it is for children to grow up in supportive communities and families.

There was another striking similarity among the risk studies: children and teens who grew up with only one or two of these challenges were not that different from those who grew up with no adversity at all. However, in every study, young people who experienced three or more of these challenges were much more likely to struggle or even fail as adults. This suggests that young people can tolerate a few hardships as they are growing up, but they are much less able to tolerate multiple hardships, piled one on top of the other.

Fortunately, after their studies had been in process for several years, the researchers began to ask another very important question. Even though many children living with three or more risk factors were not succeeding, a few children were. These were the *resilient* children who were successful in spite of the odds. The researchers began to ask, "What were the differences between these resilient children and the high risk children who failed?" Going back to the meticulous records that they had kept about the children's early years, the researchers identified two sets of characteristics that fostered resilience in children—characteristics of their families and communities and characteristics of the children themselves. The results are shown in Table 1.2. Notice that some factors that predict resilience are characteristics of the children—their abilities to seek out and make friends, beliefs that they have some control over what happens to them, their commitment to achieve, and their active participation in the community around them. Still, other important factors predicting childhood resilience were, once again, characteristics of the families and communities: the parenting skills in their families, opportunities for children to form close bonds with at least one parent and with other adults in the community, the availability of youth organizations, and effective schools.

These results show that even very high-risk children can succeed if they have ample resources and support in their community and families. Schools have a particularly important role to play in promoting the life success of high-risk children in schools

Table 1.1
Summary of Risk Conditions and Subsequent Adolescent or Adult Outcomes

Conditions of Risk	Adolescent/Adult Outcomes
• poverty	• increased delinquency/criminal activity
• low parent education	• lowered measured intelligence
• marital discord or family dysfunction	• increased educational and learning problems
• ineffective parenting	• increased likelihood of physical and mental
• child maltreatment	health problems
• poor physical health of child or parent	• increased likelihood of teenage parenthood
• parent mental illness or incapacity	• increased likelihood of unemployment
• large family size	• decreased likelihood of social competence

From Doll and Lyon, 1998.

Table 1.2
Summary of Resilience Characteristics of Children and Youth

Characteristics of Children	Characteristics of Families and Communities
• Positive social orientation	• Close bond with one caretaker
• Friendships	• Effective parenting
• Internal locus of control	• Nurturing by other adults
• Positive self-concept	• Positive adult models
• Achievement orientation	• Connections with prosocial organizations
• Community engagement	• Effective schools

From Doll and Lyon, 1998.

(Doll & Lyon, 1998; Doll et al., 2004). Schools are the second most important caretaker in children's lives, and especially when children are living with very limited resources at home, schools fill the gap between what their students have and what they need to be successful. All adults who work in schools can become the positive adult models and nurturing caretakers that contribute to children's resilience. Because of their many opportunities to talk with children about their present lives and their future dreams, school librarians have a special opportunity to create these supportive environments within a school.

WHAT MAKES SCHOOLS EFFECTIVE?

In the past two decades, educational researchers have worked to identify the characteristics of schools where children can be more successful academically, socially, and personally. Their careful analysis of school learning has shown that children's social and emotional bonds with the school are as important for their learning as the quality of instruction and curriculum (Wang, Haertel, & Walberg, 1990). The simplest explanation is that children at school need to be present, paying attention, and interested in learning before they can benefit from the instructional activities of the school. Researchers call this *school engagement,* and they report that engaging schools share certain characteristics (National Research Council and the Institute of Medicine, 2004). Not surprisingly, these characteristics duplicate the factors that predict youth resilience (Doll et al., 2004). They include the following:

- Students are able to see themselves as competent and effective learners, i.e., academic efficacy.
- Students set and work toward self-selected learning goals.
- Students behave appropriately and adaptively with a minimum of adult supervision.
- There are caring and authentic relationships between students and teachers or other adults.
- Students have ongoing and rewarding friendships with their classmates.

- Families know about and strengthen the learning that occurs in the class-room.

While an understanding of resilience has developed within school mental health, little work has been done to transfer this knowledge to the school library.

HOW WILL THIS BOOK HELP?

The purpose of this book is to help school librarians understand resilience and suggest ways to create a climate in the school library that will enable all children and teens to be resilient. A chapter is devoted to each of the six characteristics of schools where students are academically engaged, and further discussion and exploration of the research pertaining to that element is presented, followed by specific suggestions of ways to support and promote that element of resilience in the school library. The final section explores some action research techniques to document the changes that occur because of actions taken to enhance resilience.

While the focus often appears to be on troubled children or teens, it is important to remember that the six characteristics of resilient schools are helpful for all students. It is true, though, that troubled students show the largest gains in learning when these characteristics of their schools are strengthened (National Research Council and the Institute of Medicine, 2004). Still, policies, procedures, and strategies created to promote resilience benefit all students, not just those with problems. This approach strengthens pedagogy in general and enables school librarians to create a learning environment structured to help students learn to succeed.

For example, one element of resilience is a caring adult in the child's or teen's life. It goes without saying that school librarians work with children and teens. By taking the time to learn names, visit with kids, comment on clothing, or talk about the current pop stars, the school librarian demonstrates caring. It is possible the school librarian will never know how many students have been positively influenced by a supportive, positive approach. However, thinking back over your own life, how many teachers or librarians had a positive influence on you? And, how many did you thank for this caring?

While working to create a resilient school library, it is important to remember that school librarians are not alone. Instead, they are working in a learning community that involves other professionals, and many of them are as concerned about the children and teens as are school librarians. Instead of working alone, it is often useful to take a more holistic view of the student in the school and the learning support available to that student, especially those students who are troubled. Christenson and Anderson (2002) suggest seeking answers to questions like these when working with troubled students:

- "Is there a mismatch in instruction for the student?
- When was there a good match in instruction in the student's school experiences and what was that like?
- What interventions have been tried and what was the outcome?
- Does the student's attitude, in-class behavior, motivation, or use of study skills vary from subject to subject or from teacher to teacher?

- Under what conditions does the student try the hardest?
- Are there holes or missing pieces in the student's education because of attendance problems, changing schools or deviation from the intended curriculum?" (p. 389)

While it is beneficial when the whole school community is actively involved in creating an environment to promote resilience, it is not mandatory. It is still possible and beneficial for the school librarian to implement changes to enhance resilience unilaterally. The essential ingredients are an understanding of resilience, willingness to work to enhance resilience in the school library, and a desire to help students. This book provides the information needed to begin.

REFERENCES

Christenson, S. L., & Anderson, A. R. (2002). Commentary: The centrality of the learning for students' academic enabler skills. *School Psychology Review, 31*, 378–94.

Doll, B., & Lyon, M. A. (1998). Risk and resilience: Implications for the delivery of educational and mental health services in schools. *School Psychology Review, 27*, 348–63.

Doll, B., Zucker, S., & Brehm, K. (2004). *Resilient classrooms: Creating healthy environments for learning.* New York: The Guilford Press.

National Research Council and the Institute of Medicine. (2004). *Engaging schools: Fostering high school students' motivation to learn.* Committee on Increasing High School Students' Engagement and Motivation to Learn; Board on Children, Youth, and Families; Division of Behavioral and Social Sciences and Education. Washington, DC: The National Academies Press.

Wang, M. C., Haertel, G. D., & Walberg, H. J. (1990). What influences learning? A content analysis of review literature. *Journal of Educational Research, 84*, 30–43.

Werner, E. E. (2006). What can we learn about resilience from large-scale longitudinal studies? In S. Goldstein & R. B. Brooks (Eds.), *Handbook of resilience in children* (pp. 91–105). New York: Springer.

2

Evaluating the Effectiveness of Resilience Plans

It is vitally important to gather information that allows the school librarian to judge how effective the resilience activities have been. Implementing steps to improve resilience without evaluating the effectiveness of those steps is similar to teaching children how to spell without ever checking to see whether or not they are truly learning the words.

There are two main types of evaluation: informal and formal. Informal evaluation is done without a specific plan and is often based on simple impressions or observations. This type of information can be interesting, but its utility is inherently limited because of its casual nature. At the same time, informal ongoing evaluation is an important part of the feedback loop that experienced teachers and supervisors use. Many of the techniques described in this chapter could be used informally to provide quick information on how things are going in the school library. In later chapters, discussions of each type of resilience include additional suggestions for informal evaluation.

Solid data and documented results are increasingly important in this era of accountability. Formal evaluation provides evidence for assessment of resilience activities and can guide the development of future activities based on the effectiveness of current ones (Johnson, 1993; Rossi, Lipsey, & Freeman, 2004). Formal data may be more appealing to administrators, parents, and others who are the audience for reports on school library activities (Doll & Brehm, 2010). This chapter suggests techniques that can be used for formal evaluation and gives specific instructions for implementing them. Each of the six chapters on resilience include an example of formal evaluation using a suggestion given in that chapter.

While it may seem to be cumbersome or even onerous to create a formal plan to assess each attempt to address resilience, it is important to conduct formal assessments regularly, and the process will become smoother with practice. Just as school librarians would not teach a lesson on Web site evaluation without planning ahead of time (articulating goals and objectives, identifying materials to be used, developing an instructional method, etc.), neither should they implement resilience activities without developing a plan to do so. In addition, just as assessing student learning is a vital part of teaching and learning, evaluation of a resilience plan is a part of this process. Lesson planning becomes familiar and more automatic with time; so will planning for and evaluating resilience. With practice, it will not be necessary to specifically write out a plan for resilience in great detail, in the same way as lesson planning becomes less detailed for master teachers.

A BRIEF EXAMPLE

First, it is important to decide what area of resilience will be targeted for improvement. It is not wise to focus on all six areas at the same time. Instead, review the six areas, and decide which one most needs to be emphasized, or identify the one that is most important to target for improvement.

Then, decide on a specific technique to be used to enhance that area of resilience. For example, a sixth-grade class may need work in strengthening peer relationships. One way to do this is to use cooperative learning techniques to create learning situations where the students work in groups (see Chapter 9). Literature circles can be an effective way to structure deliberate group interactions when the students read and discuss a particular book.

Next, the method used to enhance resilience will itself suggest techniques for gathering information about its effectiveness. For example, observation of the students participating in literature circles could be one way to see how well students are working together. Are students engaged in the activity? Are students working on task? Are students looking at and talking to each other as appropriate? What indications are there to evaluate the quality of the interaction? Using a simple checklist, it is possible to quickly record the observations for later analysis and comparison to similar observations made before the students were assigned to literature circles or before they had experience working in these groups.

Finally, based the observations, it is possible to answer the questions: Is working in literature circles strengthening peer relationships? If so, in what ways? What are the next steps? Will literature circles continue to be part of the school library strategies? Do students need to know more about how to work in literature circles, or do they just need more time to practice? Is additional intervention is necessary? If so, what should be tried next? Is there something happening here that should be shared with teachers or administrators?

A PLANNING TEMPLATE

The previous example is a very quick description of how to gather information. However, it is too brief and too limited to fully address the effectiveness of all resilience plans. For that reason, this chapter presents a model or template to use in planning for and evaluating actions taken to enhance resilience in the school library. Each following chapter uses the same template to provide additional examples. Many people find it useful to use a step-by-step guide to evaluation, especially in the beginning until they are more familiar with techniques and more comfortable with procedures that can be used to gather and analyze data. A blank copy of the template for action research is included in the appendix. This chapter follows the template steps and provides information under each step.

PLANNING FOR RESILIENCE: HOW CAN I FIND OUT?

I. **Scenario** (Here I describe the situation that is the issue; that I am worried about, etc.)

The first step is to articulate the situation that is problematic or the area of concern. While there are many situations in a school library that could be appropriate for attention, it is impossible to address all of them at the same time. Therefore, it is important for each resilience plan to focus on only one area. In cases where it is important to work on resilience in several areas or for several grades, it is important to create a resilience plan for each area, instead of trying to do one plan for all of them at once. For example, if peer relationships with fifth graders and self-efficacy with second graders both need to be addressed, there should be two separate plans.

II. **Resilience Area and Activities** (Here I decide which area of resilience to focus on and how to do that.)

There are six areas of resilience discussed in this book. It is important to identify the area(s) that will be the focus of a particular plan. The six areas are:

1. academic efficacy (Chapter 3)

2. self-selected learning goals (Chapter 4)

3. behavioral self-control (Chapter 5)

4. strong relationships with adults (Chapter 6)

5. appropriate peer relationships (Chapter 7)

6. family involvement with the school (Chapter 8)

Once a general area of resilience has been identified, it is time to select an activity or procedure to use to enhance the area of resilience chosen. Each area of resilience is discussed in more detail in this book's chapters, and suggestions for ways to address each area are included. Based on knowledge of a particular school and particular students, one or more of the suggestions given in this book may be identified or modified. Experienced colleagues can be used as resources and support. Or, based on the information given in this book, another approach to increasing or supporting resilience may be devised.

III. **Question** (What is the main question I need to answer to decide whether or not the technique I chose is enhancing resilience?)

The next step is to decide what information is needed to determine whether or not the resilience activity chosen is successful. To identify the type of information needed, think about what kinds of results or behavior will show whether or not the resilience activity has made a difference. For example, if a parent book club is started to strengthen family involvement in the school library, what will show whether or not that book club is successful? What should parental participation in this book club accomplish? Questions that may help focus the data gathering include:

- Am I mainly interested in having parents join the club and come to meetings? Why? What would that tell me?

- Am I interested in the quality of the discussions? Again, why is this important? What would it tell me about support for student resilience?

- Do I want to know what effect the book club has on the parent–child relationship? If this is my main question, how would knowing this help me analyze the success of the book club? Or, what would this tell me about how families support the school and school activities?

- Do I want to know whether students who have a parent in the book club have a more positive view of the school library than those who do not? Again, the question is how would knowing this help me understand how the book club affected the relationship between the family and the school library?

The questions that are important will identify appropriate methods for gathering the information needed to assess the success of the project. It is important to clarify the questions that will be addressed to understand why the chosen activity was implemented. This step clarifies and provides focus to the project at an early stage to ensure well-designed activities.

IV. **Methodology** (How will I gather information to answer the question?)

Once the question that needs to be answered has been identified, I will think about how to answer that question.

A. **What information do I need to gather?**

The first step is to identify the kind of information needed in order to assess the success of the activity. In the book club example described previously, the goal for the book club suggests the types of data needed to assess its success. For example:

- If parent participation is important, attendance figures can provide that information.

- If the quality of the discussions is the focus of concern, it is necessary to analyze and record the content of the discussions.

- If the impact that the book club has had on the parent–child relationship is most important, information about what happens between parents and their children is needed—and this is something that may not be directly observable.

- If the effect the book club might have on student perceptions of or interactions with the school library is an area of concern, it will be necessary to gather information describing student behaviors and student reactions.

B. **How might I gather that information?**

After considering the kinds of information needed to answer the questions that were identified, it is time to decide on a method for gathering that information. There are several standard methods used to gather information, and one or more might be appropriate for a given situation.

1. Use **existing records** or information.

   There is information available in existing records, such as circulation records or student standardized test scores. For example, if the impact of the book club on the school library is important, circulation records from before and after the book club discussions of particular books could indicate whether they circulate more after being discussed. This is one way to assess the impact the book club is having on student use of the school library.

2. **Observe** what is happening.

   While working with students and teachers and parents, it is often possible to observe what is happening. Sometimes, observation can be used to gather information about how well activities are going. One advantage to observation is that it is possible to record what people are actually doing, instead of what they say they are doing. It is important to think in advance of the types of behaviors that might occur and then construct a check sheet or other form to record observations. For example, if the quality of the book club discussions is the focus of the observations, it is possible to create an observation instrument with columns to check off the types of questions and responses:

   • informational questions and responses calling for simple recall of information;

   • thought questions and responses requiring thoughtful interpretation of something in the book;

   • analysis questions and responses based on careful evaluation of some element of the book; or

   • critical questions and responses based on deep thinking and application of something in the book to another situation.

   A column for exchanges that do not focus on the book may also be added. Data recorded in this way can be easy to work with later when analyzing the data.

3. Another option is to **gather information** from people directly. There are several ways to do this.

   a. **Interview** (large group, small group, individual, or telephone)

      In an interview, people are asked to respond to a prepared set of questions. It is important to prepare questions in advance to ensure that everything is included in the interview. And, when conducting more than one interview, the list of questions ensures that everyone is asked the same questions.

If the interviewer meets with more than one person at a time, it is possible to get more information and more creative responses as the interviewees listen to and interact with each other. Comments from one person could change the comments offered by other individuals. At the same time, if the people being interviewed don't like each other, this dynamic can have a negative impact on the interview.

With an interview, it is possible to explain questions that interviewees don't understand and to ask follow-up questions based on their responses.

Also, in a face-to-face interview situation, the respondents may feel they have to give "correct" answers instead of feeling free to offer their true feelings.

It is time consuming to conduct interviews, especially if a lot of people will be interviewed, either individually or in small groups. Sometimes telephone interviews are a useful substitute, especially if the people being asked to respond are scattered throughout the geographic area or are available at different times of the day or week.

It is beneficial to conduct a couple of interviews to practice questions and to learn the kinds of responses that are likely. This information can be used to refine the questions for later interviews. Or, this input could be used to prepare a written questionnaire to send to everyone in the target group. (See point b below.)

Interviews can be the best way to get some types of information. For example, if the impact the book club has had on the parent–child relationship is important, it might be best to ask the parent for this information directly in an interview.

b. **Questionnaire**

A survey or questionnaire is a prepared set of questions used to ask respondents for information that solicits written feedback. Questions may be either closed (i.e., with limited responses, such as "Did you come to the school library last week?") or open (i.e., without a set of predetermined responses, e.g., "Talk about why you enjoy or don't enjoy coming to the school library.") Closed questions are easier to quantify when analyzing the responses, but open questions can sometimes give more information or unanticipated information.

It is important to write a first draft of the questions and then pretest them before administering the questionnaire. Alternatively, ask someone else in the school to read the questions to make sure the questions are clear and unambiguous and give the kind of information needed.

As with interviews, respondents may give the answers they think are correct or desirable, and the information will describe what people think or say they did, not what they actually did. However, because questionnaires can be anonymous, the answers may be more truthful because the respondents feel protected.

Questionnaires are less time consuming than interviews. If they are distributed during a meeting or other event, it is possible to have a fairly high return rate. Remember that when fewer than half of the respondents return the questionnaire, those who did not answer could have given replies that totally contradict the results recorded.

There are times, however, when questionnaires and surveys are a preferred way to gather information. If the focus is on the effect the book club might have on student perceptions of or feelings about the school library, it is possible to create a questionnaire to give to all students, and compare the results of students with parents in the book club with those of students whose parents do not participate. (To maintain anonymity, ask students whether or not their parents participate.)

c. **Test**
Another way to evaluate the effectiveness of resilience activities is to give a test. Tests are frequently used in educational settings, especially given the present emphasis on standardized testing. Tests can be multiple choice, short answer, essay, open book, or any myriad configurations.

Tests are more appropriate for some purposes than others. For example, a test would not give useful information about the parent book club. However, a test would be a useful measure of learning for a lesson that focuses on teaching students to conduct a Web search and evaluate Web sites using a step-by-step model. This approach might strengthen students' academic efficacy, increasing their ability to recognize and apply an approach to locating quality information on the Web. In this case, a test might indicate whether or not the student can recall the steps in the correct order; still, this would not show whether or not students can use the steps. When students are asked to actually locate an appropriate source, tests can indicate whether or not students can do this, but they may not indicate which methods they used. Thus, it is important to be sure that what students are tested on matches the skill or knowledge they have learned and also gives useful information. For example, asking students to recognize correctly spelled words in a list is not the same skill as being able to correctly spell the words themselves.

d. **Assignment or Exercise**
A test is not the only way to evaluate student skills or knowledge. Sometimes it is more effective to ask the student to complete an assignment using the newly acquired skills. Another option is to give students an opportunity to practice the skill in class immediately

following instruction, while observing how well students are able to perform the task.

The advantage of assignments and exercises is that they allow students to use the skills or knowledge just taught and are usually less stressful than testing. Be sure that the assignment or exercise matches the content of the lesson that was taught. The intent of the activity is to verify the effectiveness of the lesson taught, not to focus on other material.

Again, this technique is not appropriate for the parent book club because the parents were not being instructed on specific skills; however, it could work well with a lesson on Web searching and evaluation. For example, after teaching the students the steps involved in searching the Web, students could work individually or in pairs to locate several Web sites using the step-by-step procedure that was just taught. An exercise sheet listing the steps could be used to guide student efforts. Students could also be given an assignment to use this same procedure after the lesson was over, or they could be asked to locate three Web sites using the procedure that was taught and explain why those sites are appropriate for their topic.

C. **Collect the data.**

Using whichever of these techniques is appropriate, it is time to locate the existing data, conduct the interview, administer the questionnaire, give the test, or hand out the assignment or exercise. Once the data have been collected, it is time to go on to the next step of data analysis.

V. **Data Analysis**

Once the raw data have been gathered—that is, the numbers, the answers to the questions, the information about the students—it is time to analyze the data to find any patterns or information lurking within it. Different types of data require different approaches.

A. **Numbers**

There are several options available for data expressed as numbers. Any or all of them may be appropriate. Selection of the "best" method often depends on the nature of the data and the purpose for which the data have been collected.

1. **Frequencies**

When the number of items in a category have been counted, a frequency distribution can be an effective way to find overall patterns in the information. For example, if the number of parents who came to the first, second, third, and fourth book club meetings is known, a frequency distribution can help find new information in the numbers. For a frequency distribution, first list all of the options, numbers, or categories available, and then figure out how many responses, books, people, or whatever are in each category. For the example of book club attendance, list the meeting and then the number of parents who attended that meeting:

first meeting	10
second meeting	11
third meeting	4
fourth meeting	10

Once the numbers are distributed, it is time to understand why particular results occurred. The figures seem to show a steady attendance, except for the third week. Maybe there was a community event that night, or perhaps bad weather kept people at home. But overall, steady attendance could indicate that the parent book club meets a community need, and the fact that parents attend strengthens the tie between the home and the school library.

While this is a simple example for demonstration purposes, a frequency distribution can be very useful to identify patterns when large numbers of data points are involved.

2. **Bar graphs**
Once a frequency distribution has been created, it is often useful to create a bar graph or histogram based on the data in that frequency distribution. In effect, a bar graph makes a "picture" of the data. For some people and purposes, a pictorial version of the data makes some patterns easier to recognize and understand. Spreadsheet programs, such as the Microsoft Excel program used in Figure 2.1, can be used to create the bar graphs.

Frequency distributions, and their corresponding bar graphs, can also identify and represent patterns in such diverse information as the number of responses in various categories, or the number of "yes" or "no" answers. To create a bar graph, it is necessary to "count" the number of items in each group.

3. **Percentages**
Another way to analyze data is to calculate percentages. Percentages can be calculated for all members of a group or all cases that are represented, and the total can be described as "100 percent." For example, because you know the total number of times parents attended the book club, it is possible to calculate the percentage of the attendance that occurred each week. It is not possible to calculate percentages for an open-ended category or categories, or when it is not possible to compute an overall total or the number of items in each category. For example, in order to use percentages to determine the effect of book club participation on students, it is necessary to have data from all students of parents in the club, not just those students who voluntarily talk with

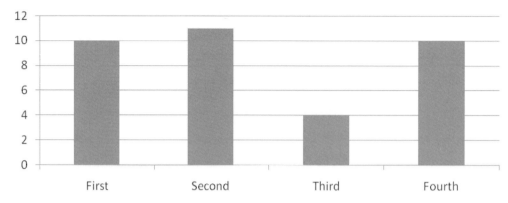

Figure 2.1: Parents attending book club meetings.

the school librarian about the book club. To calculate a percentage, divide the number of items in a particular category by the overall total of all items in all categories, and multiply by 100.

$$\frac{\text{number of items in the category}}{\text{total number of items in all categories}} \times 100$$

For example, the following figures represent book talk attendance, where the first column identifies the meeting and the second column lists the number of attendees:

first	10
second	11
third	4
fourth	10

Using this hypothetical situation, the following percentages would be calculated:

first	29%	(10 divided by 35 times 100)
second	31%	(11 divided by 35 times 100)
third	11%	(4 divided by 35 times 100)
fourth	29%	(10 divided by 35 times 100)

Percentages show the relative weight or value of one category compared to another. This is especially useful when there are large frequencies.

4. **Pie graph**
   Pie graphs are particularly effective in providing a pictorial representation of percentages. Because the figures add to 100 percent (give or take some effects of rounding), the pie or circle graph does a nice job of showing the relative size of each "slice of the pie." Again, spreadsheet

programs can be used to create the graph. Figure 2.2 is based on the percentages calculated for the parent book club attendance.

5. **Change over time**
   When it is important to understand the way something that has changed over time, a line graph can be very useful to show trends. To construct a line graph, the data must be available in numbers that can be mapped onto the vertical axis of the graph. The horizontal axis of the graph usually represents time (dates, sequence, or prices), although this is not always the case. Using the data from the book club attendance recorded previously, the line graph would look like Figure 2.3.

   Obviously, this chart clearly emphasizes the decrease in attendance at the third meeting. This visual display shows change more dramatically than the bar graph for the parent attendance data.

B. **Observations**
   Some of the data gathered will be observations made of students, teachers, or parents.

1. **Group into categories**
   The first step in analyzing observation data is to group the observations into categories. If the observations are based on a check sheet or other instrument, this categorization can go fairly quickly. For example, the types of comments recorded for the book club discussions may be grouped into four categories: informational, thought, analysis, or critical. The results of this analysis are listed in the following two columns, where the first column describes the type of question and the second column lists the number of occurrences:

Type of Question	Number of Responses
informational	78
thought	93
analysis	48
critical	32

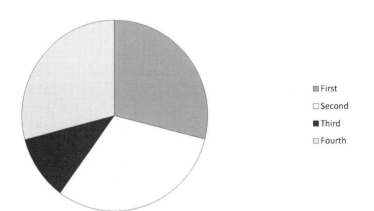

■ First
□ Second
■ Third
□ Fourth

Figure 2.2: Attendance at meetings.

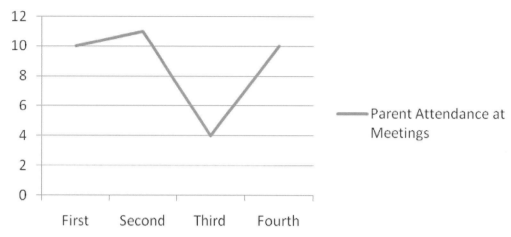

Figure 2.3 Parent attendance at meetings.

Then, it is possible to calculate the percentage of responses and questions in each category, using the technique discussed previously. For the data on questions and responses at the book club discussions, the following percentages were calculated:

Type of Question	% of Responses
informational	31%
thought	37%
analysis	19%
critical	13%

Percentages show the relative weight or value of one category compared to another. This is especially useful when there are large frequencies.

2. **Charts or graphs**

   Once some of the patterns in the data have been found, it is appropriate to create charts or graphs to give a "picture" of the data. In this example, a pie graph is appropriate because the responses total 100 percent. Figure 2.4 is based on the percentages calculated for type of parent responses from the parent book club discussions.

C. **Interviews and Questionnaires**

1. **Closed questions**

   Closed questions provide the respondents a limited number of responses to choose from. This makes it easier to handle the data. For example, one question on the survey for parents in the book club might be, "How many children do you have attending this school?" And several response options will follow, such as "one," "two," or "three or more."

Once all questionnaires have been collected, the data can be collated and either tables or charts can be created, depending on the characteristics of the data and intended uses for it. For example, for the parents in the book club, a table could look like this:

Number of Children	Number of Responses
One	3 (27%)
Two	6 (55%)
Three or more	2 (18%)

Data from other sources show that more than 50 percent of the students in the school are the only child from their families enrolled in the school. Looking at this data, only 27 percent of the parents participating in the book club have only one child in the school. Obviously, for this group, parents with multiple children in the school are disproportionately represented. It is necessary to investigate further to determine what this means for this particular school.

2. **Open questions—try to group into categories and/or find trends**
   Sometimes the information from questionnaires or interviews comes from open-ended questions that yield diverse but hard-to-classify data. Then it is important to read the responses closely, create categories, and develop criteria for each category. For example, a question asking parents to discuss their reaction to the book club may result in a wide range of responses, both positive and negative. Possible responses may include:

   - I love being able to discuss these books with my daughter.

   - I am so glad to be reading books my son may be reading.

   - Reading these books has enabled my son and I to discuss some of the issues raised in the book without personalizing the discussion.

   - I am really impressed with the quality of the writing in the books we are reading.

■ Information

▨ Thought

▨ Analysis

■ Critical

Figure 2.4 Question/response types.

- It is so nice to get out of the house once a month and talk with other adults.

- I am more worried than ever about today's kids if these books reflect the realities of their lives.

To analyze these responses, read the responses, find patterns, and create a classification system that best conveys in a short form the information contained in these surveys. Specific quotes can be used to illustrate the discussion of the survey results. Be sure to include all perspectives, in fairness to all the individuals involved. For example, the feedback above may be grouped into two main categories—positive comments (five of them) and negative comments (one). There are also three comments relating the act of reading these books to the parent–child relationship, one about the quality of the literature, and one person just enjoys the conversation.

VI. **What does this tell me about my original question?**

Once the data have been analyzed, it is time to examine the results in terms of the outcomes or indicators of success that were formulated as a part of the original plan. Based on what was learned or observed, decide the following:

A. How will this help me make decisions or better understand resilience in my school library?

B. Should I continue the current activity, make changes to the current activity, or devise and implement another activity.

C. Was the resilience plan a success? If so, why do I believe it succeeded? If not, how would I recommend revising the plan?

VII. Using the Information

Once I have looked at the results, it is time to use the information for further planning. I need to let the principal know that parents did come to the book discussions and that they indicated the books helped them interact more with their children. Also, it is time to decide what to do next. Much of the information is positive, so I will continue it next year.

CLASSMAPS SURVEY FOR SCHOOL LIBRARIES

Trying to decide where to begin to foster student resilience can be overwhelming, and it may be difficult to identify one or more of the resilience areas that should be the focus of efforts to improve resilience. One important tool to help with either task is the ClassMaps Survey for School Libraries. The ClassMaps Survey for School Libraries can also be used to help evaluate the success of activities implemented to improve resilience in the school library.

ClassMaps Survey for School Libraries consists of 50 questions grouped into 8 categories that ask students to respond to statements about themselves, their classmates, and their school librarian and/or teacher. Given four options, students select the one that corresponds most closely with their belief or behavior. The four options are "never," "sometimes," "often," and "almost always." It is possible to administer the whole ClassMaps Survey for School Libraries, or to identify one segment that will be most helpful.

The ClassMaps Survey for School Libraries is adopted from the ClassMaps Survey 2007 (Doll, Spies, LeClair, Kurien, & Foley, 2010; Doll et al., 2009), which was created to provide working educational professionals a valid and reliable instrument that could be used by busy teachers to effectively identify classroom practices that either enhanced or hindered student performance. One author of this book (Beth Doll) has led the work to design and validate this instrument for classroom teachers. The survey's original content was carefully planned from a comprehensive review of developmental research describing the correlates of students' school success (Doll, Zucker, & Brehm, 2004), and it was refined in a series of studies with elementary and middle-aged students so that items were written in clear and straightforward language and scale reliability was strengthened (Doll et al., in press). Evidence that the surveys factor into the predicted subscales and have strong internal consistency reliabilities (.79 to .93) is summarized in Doll et al. (2004), Doll et al. (2009), and Doll et al. (2010). To accommodate the ClassMaps Survey 2007 for use in school libraries, minor changes were made in the survey's wording to reflect the realities of a school library setting.

CONCLUSION

While it is important to evaluate the effectiveness of resilience plans being implemented, that process need not be intimidating. Evaluation is an ongoing part of being a school librarian. The purpose of this chapter was to suggest some tools to help gather appropriate information to use in assessing the resilience plans that may be implemented.

REFERENCES

Doll, B., & Brehm, K. (2010). *Resilient playgrounds*. New York: Routledge.

Doll, B., Kurien, S., LeClair, C., Spies, R., Champion, A., & Osborn, A. (2009). The ClassMaps Survey: A framework for promoting positive classroom environments. In R. Gilman, S. Huebner, and M. Furlong (Eds.), *Handbook of positive psychology in the schools* (pp. 213–227). New York: Routledge.

Doll, B., Spies, R. A., LeClair, C., Kurien, S., & Foley, B. P. (2010). Student perceptions of classroom learning environments: Development of the ClassMaps Survey. *School Psychology Review, 39*, 203–218.

Doll, B., Zucker, S., & Brehm, K. (2004). *Resilient classrooms*. New York: Guilford.

Johnson, B. (1993). *Teacher-as-researcher*. ERIC Digest. Washington, DC: Eric Clearinghouse on Teacher Education. ED 355205.

Rossi, P. H., Lipsey, M. W., & Freeman, H. E. (2004). *Evaluation: A systematic approach* (7th ed.). Thousand Oaks, CA: Sage.

3

Academic Efficacy

At its core, academic efficacy is students' belief that they can succeed in school; or, in the often-quoted words of Henry Ford, "If you think you can or you think you can't, you're right." Students who *know* that they can succeed act differently than students who expect to fail—they try harder, persist longer, use tricks and strategies when struggling with difficult tasks, and ask for help when they need it. Alternatively, students who expect to fail are reluctant to try tasks that they think are difficult, put less effort into their work, give up quickly, and sometimes even misbehave in order to escape schoolwork that overwhelms them.

For example, imagine a young man opening an unfamiliar book in the school library. If he believes that he cannot read, he may page through the book, look for pictures, count the number of pages, and put the book down, selecting instead a much easier and not very challenging book to check out. Often, these students do not check out books unless someone else requires that they do. Compare this to another young man who is quite confident in his reading. He might pick up an unfamiliar book, leaf through several chapters, read a few paragraphs here and there, and try to decide if the book is interesting and fun to read. This second student might be bored with books that are simple or predictable and will look instead for a favorite author or for something challenging to read. Students' efficacy for reading is particularly important for their behavior in the school library.

Interestingly, one of the most prominent psychologists studying efficacy is Albert Bandura (1969), whose earlier work described the principles of behavior modification and their application in school, clinic, and laboratory settings. His research demonstrated that even after controlling for the antecedents and consequences of human behavior, it was clear that additional variations in behavior were due to a person's understanding, attitudes, and beliefs about the purpose and results of the behavior. As Bandura (1993) states, "Most human motivation is cognitively generated. People motivate themselves and guide their actions anticipatorily by the exercise of forethought. They form beliefs about what they can do. They anticipate likely outcomes of prospective actions. They set goals for themselves and plan courses of action designed to realize valued futures" (p. 128). One of the most important things teachers and school librarians can do for students is strengthen their efficacy so that students know that they will be successful in school.

HOW IS ACADEMIC EFFICACY FORMED?

The most common explanation of academic efficacy is that students who have often succeeded in the past expect to succeed, while students who have often failed in the past will expect to continue failing. Researchers agree, and their studies have shown that students' past learning history is the most important cause of their academic efficacy beliefs (Pajares, 1996). Students will be most efficacious when they have a history of succeeding at moderately difficult tasks (Bandura, 1997). Experiences with success on very easy tasks are not highly valued by students, but neither are experiences with tasks so difficult that the students can only complete them with lots of help from other people. In many cases, very difficult tasks can be adjusted by breaking them into steps and teaching students strategies that help them organize or understand the task. These kinds of assistance make it possible for students to complete challenging tasks independently, and so build efficacy.

Still, past learning history is not the only source of students' academic efficacy. Four other important sources are:

- Persuasion from adults. Students expect to succeed when adults (teachers, parents, and school librarians) tell them that they will succeed. Confidence from adults is convincing.

- Persuasion from peers. Classmates also contribute to students' efficacy when they express confidence in their peers' abilities, and their confidence is even more convincing when it is heartfelt and specific.

- Examples of successful classmates. When students see that other students much like themselves are succeeding, they expect to be successful, too. Examples of success are even more potent when students notice the successes of their classmates, often because a nearby adult has pointed out and celebrated the success.

- Emotional well-being. Students are predisposed to success when they feel content and happy and predisposed to failure when they feel unhappy or angry.

These additional explanations are important because they describe characteristics of the school's social environment or climate that are important for students' academic efficacy.

Persuasive comments that adults make about students' task performance are especially valuable because, next to parents, adults in schools are the most visible people in children's lives (Schunk & Pajares, 2005). The most beneficial persuasive comments are more than simple compliments or kind statements. To be truly effective, persuasion must be specific, true, and believable. Examples include a school librarian telling a student, "I'm impressed with how carefully you're reading; you'll be quite an expert in the history of trains." or "You certainly understand how to search through the Web—you're finding out the exact source of each reference. I'm glad that you're helping us answer these questions." Importantly, these examples are comments that describe the students' strategies (finding the exact source) or effort (reading carefully). These types of feedback are not only specific and believable but also help students notice what they are doing that is notable. Effort and strategies are under the ready control of students, and they realistically expect that they can repeat their success in the future by giving good effort or using good strategies. In contrast, comments about students' abilities ("You're really good at surfing the Web.") are not very helpful when students are first learning a task because they may not find them to be believable. Ability comments are only useful once it is clear that students have mastered a skill, and they know that they have.

Persuasion from other students is also important. Students learn to notice and make positive comments about each others' success by imitating adults. The admiration of peers is particularly convincing because students value the social status that it represents and because classmates are usually well-informed about the nature and difficulty of the tasks that they are learning. Unfortunately, left to their own devices, students are likely to make joking or derogatory comments about each others' performance. Still, they can be prompted to change the things they say to each other. For example, one school librarian had a rule that whenever she caught students saying something negative about other students, they had to say two positive things to "pay" for the harm they had caused. Importantly, this sense of competence is contagious across students in a class so that when a majority of students within a classroom expect to be successful, their confidence rubs off on their classmates.

Peers and teachers also represent important vicarious models of efficacy and competence. In some ways, peers are the most believable models because students expect adults to be more competent than themselves (Schunk & Pajares, 2005), but they expect to match the competence of many of their peers. For example, a thick and heavy book (such as those in the Harry Potter series) might totally overwhelm some children until they notice that their friends and classmates are reading the book and enjoying it. Then, in simple terms, seeing someone very much like themselves master that book is convincing evidence that they, too, are likely to succeed. Adults can also model efficacy for their students by acting out ways to cope with difficult work. For example, students might observe the school librarian page through a book and hear the school librarian softly comment, "Wow, this is a long book. It might take me a long time to read it. But, I think it looks pretty interesting. I've always wanted to know more about how the human body works. I bet I could read it if I worked at it." The school librarian has become a model for coping with an unfamiliar or difficult task and students can imitate the adults by thinking carefully about a new task but recognizing that effort and persistence can overcome the difficulty.

The sense of emotional well-being that students bring with them each morning is not always under the control of adults in a school. However, schools can create calming and comfortable settings for their students, and adults can acknowledge students' jagged feelings and provide simple reassurance. Alternatively, school environments that are uncomfortable and irritating can feed students' sense of frustration, detract from their concentration, and predispose them to be pessimistic about their own abilities.

What can school librarians do to help? Specific strategies can be taught to students to help them become better learners. Even once the strategies are taught and practiced, students may need reminders to use them. By being aware of these sources of efficacy, teachers and school librarians can help students learn how to become successful learners, and so increase their self-confidence. As Zimmerman and Kitsantas (2005) noted, "people's self-efficacy beliefs about their self-regulatory competence proved to be predictive of not only their use of self-regulatory processes but also their learning and performance outcomes" (p. 523).

SUGGESTIONS

Self-Instruction

Seifert and Wheeler (1994) suggest teaching students a self-instruction approach to help them develop an organized strategy for learning. One technique might be to help students break a task down into discrete steps. For example, if a student needs to find a good Web site for a high school seismology lesson, the activity could be broken down into these steps:

1. Identify a Web site on seismology.

   a. Write down possible search terms (e.g., seismology, earthquake).
   b. Select a term to use.
   c. Decide which search engine to use (Google, Ask Jeeves, etc.).
   d. Conduct the search with the selected term and search engine.
   e. Select a site from the list of hits.

2. Determine the quality of the Web site by checking:

   a. Authority
   b. Authorship
   c. Bias
   d. Usability
   e. Appropriateness

3. Decide whether to use this site, or return to Step 1e and select another site.
4. Repeat until a satisfactory site is identified.

Besides integrating this step-by-step instruction into lessons, it is a good idea to provide students with a handout showing the steps, and post the steps close to the computers so students can readily refer to them while researching.

There can be several ways to evaluate the success of this technique. One is to observe students to see how many of them are following the steps, how many show increasing independence in following the steps, and how many still need help. The goal is to enable students to become independent users and to help them understand that they can follow this procedure successfully. Be ready to provide support as needed. Also, it is possible to assess the quality of the final product (e.g., a paper or a PowerPoint) to determine whether or not the students were able to locate appropriate sites.

Another issue in self-efficacy is teaching the student to identify the cause of failures that might occur. Some students who already display a robust sense of self-efficacy realize that insufficient effort or using the wrong strategy might have caused the failure. However, some students who are not confident in their ability may blame themselves and believe that they are too dumb or too stupid to do the task. For example, students who quit at Step 1e may not find an appropriate site, but the failure would be due to the fact that the process was not completed and that the students stopped work without an evaluation of the site. It is important for students to realize that failure did not occur because they cannot learn but because they did not complete the entire set of steps necessary for success. Another type of failure could occur if the wrong procedure is used. For example, students might be asked to compare a book to its video. In this case, a Web site might not have the appropriate information, but the failure would be due to use of an inappropriate strategy (one devised for evaluation of Web sites instead of comparison of print and video). In either case, the failure does not indicate that the students cannot learn, merely that they used the wrong approach. In both cases, it is important to work with the students to identify the cause of the failure. This can be done in several ways. By guiding students to review the steps that were followed, they could identify where the failure occurred and correct it to complete the assignment successfully. Teaching students to help each other is another way to help students learn to follow a sequence of steps independently. After initial instruction in the model of steps, students could be paired. (It might be appropriate to determine how to group students before they arrive to ensure that at least one student is an accomplished independent learner. Also, it may be a good idea to designate the more competent student as the one to do the activity first, to provide additional reinforcement for the slower learner.) As they go through the steps, ask the students to explain to each other what they are doing and what steps come next.

Motivation Strategies

Teachers can increase student self-efficacy by using a program of motivation strategies. Taken together, these strategies create a plan of instruction and reinforcement that helps students become stronger, more independent learners. For example, by reviewing with students skills they already have and those they will need to complete a given task or problem, school librarians can set students up to succeed. School librarians and teachers can focus on specific learning goals or techniques for students to use, provide opportunities for students to observe others use the strategies, and provide students with feedback and rewards as appropriate (Urdan & Turner, 2005).

Research has shown that when students can set or identify specific learning goals, they have greater belief in their ability to learn. One way to foster and support this is by stating explicitly at the beginning of a lesson what students should learn as a result of that lesson. For example, when working with second graders, say that today's lesson will help them understand the purpose of guide words at the top of the dictionary page and how to use them effectively. After some initial instruction, ask the students to restate the purpose of the lesson before giving them practice in identifying and using guide words. As the students work with guide words, circulate and give individual help to students who are having trouble. By reiterating the purpose of the lesson, it is possible to help some of the students refocus on the main purpose of the lesson. Then, as students correctly demonstrate their understanding of guide words, compliment them on their accomplishments, and reinforce the fact that they have successfully learned about guide words.

Another recommended approach is to teach students specific strategies to use in learning. Sources for these are the information-seeking models developed for use in schools, such as Eisenberg and Berkowitz's (1990) Big6™ or Kuhlthau's (1993) "seeking meaning" approach. These models suggest steps for students to follow in recognizing and/or identifying their need for information, searching for information to answer that need, evaluating the quality of that information, using that information to address their need or to create a product, sharing the results or product created, and then evaluating the steps they used to get there. There is no one model that is correct for every situation, but it is important to select one that is appropriate for a particular school, and incorporate it into the instructional planning and teaching done by the school librarian. This model should be infused throughout the curriculum, and teaching should return to this model repeatedly throughout the years that the student is in the school. The steps in the chosen process should be prominently displayed in the school library. Repeated instruction in and use of one model will allow the students to become familiar with it and increase chances that they will internalize the model as a guide for their own information seeking and use. Becoming familiar with the model and becoming comfortable with its use will provide students with a specific strategy to use when they need information. This will help them become comfortable with the process and have more confidence in their ability to successfully locate and use information. They will have faith in their ability to learn.

Assessment of the effectiveness of the model on student information seeking can be done in several ways. Observation of students working on research can help identify students still having trouble and students who are working independently. Examination of the final reports or projects will indicate which students were able to locate and use information effectively. This is a situation where it is better to have the students apply the model than it is to give a written test asking them to list the steps of the model.

Providing opportunities for students to observe others using various strategies is another way to help students acquire successful strategies for learning. For example, when a student asks for help finding a book, the school librarian can go with the student to the online public access catalog (OPAC); put in the search term(s); write down the author, title, and call number; and then walk with the student to the shelf to find the book. This informal instruction has been effective in high school libraries. While the school librarian seemed to spend a lot of time doing this at the beginning of the year, more and more students became independent users of the OPAC as the year progressed, and some were even helping their fellow students. Again, observation of student behavior in the school library is an effective way to determine how well the technique is working.

It is important to provide students with feedback that focuses on the strategies used to create the product, not just the final product. After teaching students how to evaluate the quality of Web sites, it is not sufficient to grade the final paper. Instead, it is important to understand how the students determined the quality of the Web site. Examining the bibliographies of final papers and rating the quality of the Web sites used in one way to approach this. Another approach is to have students explain (either on a worksheet or in an annotated bibliography) why they have confidence in the information on the Web site. Also, interactions with students while they are searching for and evaluating Web sites is another, albeit less formal, way to evaluate their ability to judge Web sites.

The final step in the program is to reward students based on their performance. In one way, the traditional grading system does this. However, it is not sufficient to rely totally on grades. Some students will flourish under this reward system; others will struggle or feel discouraged. It is important to recognize and applaud student achievement in many little ways as students work through the tasks and learning opportunities presented throughout a lesson. A student may successfully complete a project, finish a worksheet, or follow the steps to create a new PowerPoint slide. At that point, the student needs to know that the school librarian recognizes and applauds his achievement. The reward can be as simple as saying, "Good work."

Changes in the Learning Environment

Ridley and Walther (1995) have identified a number of things teachers and school librarians can do to help students become more confident learners. One thing is to give extra assistance when students need it. This may occur as the school librarian circulates while students are working on an assigned task, or it may happen during recess or after school. It is especially important to learn to know the students so it is possible to identify those who are unwilling to ask for help and take the initiative to approach them instead. While the school librarian is teaching or the students are working on their assigned tasks, it is important to closely watch what they are doing. This can help to identify students who are having trouble or to give quick reassurance to students who are uncertain about what they are doing. A quiet, nonjudgmental interest in their work enables adults to help students feel more confident about their learning.

When a student is having trouble, it is important to quietly, professionally, and kindly provide accurate detailed feedback to help the student understand both content and process mistakes. Some of this can be done in written responses on the student's work; at other times it is more useful to provide immediate feedback while the student is working.

As recommended previously, it can be useful to many students to present the material in steps. It is important for these steps to be small and to lead directly to the final product. Younger children will need smaller steps than older children because the older children have more experience and also are more advanced developmentally. Additionally, it is important to provide more than one opportunity for students to learn the material. Just as first graders are not taught 2 + 2 = 4 on Monday and never return to it again, there must be multiple opportunities for students to learn and practice the skills being taught. The school librarian will have contact with the students as long as they are in the school. This provides ample opportunity to revisit (scaffold) skills with the students to increase their learning and retention of the skills.

PLANNING FOR RESILIENCE

Based on the information in this chapter, an example follows of how to evaluate the success of a plan that has been implemented, using the template from Chapter 2.

HOW CAN I FIND OUT?

I. **Scenario** (Here I describe the situation that is the issue; that I am worried about, etc.)

I want to teach three classes of second graders the fundamentals of using the OPAC to locate materials in the school library. I also want to help them to understand that they can successfully use the OPAC. I know that it will take a lot of time, a lot of patience, and a lot of praise to do this.

II. **Resilience Area and Activities** (Here I decide which area of resilience to focus on and how to do that.)

I will focus on academic efficacy and use a teaching process that presents a step-by-step model for using the OPAC. I will also make it a point to provide a lot of positive reinforcement.

III. **Question** (What is the main question I need to answer to decide whether or not the technique I chose is enhancing resilience?)

Can I give directed positive feedback to students learning to use the OPAC? As a result of my efforts, do the second graders believe they can use the OPAC to locate materials in the school library?

IV. **Methodology** (How will I gather information to answer the question?)

A. **What information do I need to gather?**

I will need to gather two kinds of information: information about whether or not I am giving appropriate positive feedback to students engaged in searching and information about changes in the students' perception of their ability to locate materials in the school library.

B. **How might I gather that information?**

1. Use **existing records** or information.

Not appropriate in this case. There is no information currently available on whether or not the second graders believe they can use the OPAC, and there is no data available that has already been gathered on the type of feedback I have been giving the students.

2. **Observe** what is happening.

This could provide information, but it would be difficult to keep accurate records of what is happening while I am actively teaching the students. Instead, I will use a voice-activated tape recorder to document my interaction with the second graders so I don't have to interrupt my teaching to record interactions. Because it would be very time-consuming to analyze data from every class when I taught second graders to use the OPAC, I will instead make a recording of four classes—the first one, two in the middle, and the last one.

3. **Gather information** from people directly.

a. **Interview**

This could provide information, but direct personal interviews might be difficult with second graders.

b. **Questionnaire**

I will use the appropriate section of the ClassMaps Survey for School Libraries. I will give it to the students twice—when I begin teaching them about the OPAC and when I have finished. I will use the portion shown in Table 3.1.

c. **Test**

Not appropriate in this case because I am interested in whether or not students believe they can succeed, not whether they actually do or not.

d. **Assignment or Exercise**

This could work, but I am interested more in the process than in a final product that can be easily assessed through assignments.

C. **Collect the data** (using the technique I identified previously).

V. **Data Analysis** (Now what do I do with all this information?)

A. **Numbers** (not used in this case)

B. **Observations**

I have the tape recordings made while I was teaching the students to use the OPAC. I will analyze my comments to determine whether I made general comments ("You are doing a good job") or more specific comments that help students understand what they are doing correctly and why ("You are doing a good job of writing down the title of the book and the call number to help you find it on the shelf when you go to look").

Table 3.1
ClassMap Survey Academic Efficacy Portion

☐ Boy / male	☐ Girl / female	I am in the ____ grade.
Believing in Me		

1. I know how to use this school library.

Never	Sometimes	Often	Almost always

2. I can do as well as most kids in this school library.

Never	Sometimes	Often	Almost always

3. I can help other kids understand how to use the school library.

Never	Sometimes	Often	Almost always

4. I can be a very good student in this school library.

Never	Sometimes	Often	Almost always

5. I can do the hard work in this school library.

Never	Sometimes	Often	Almost always

6. I expect to do very well when I work hard in this school library.

Never	Sometimes	Often	Almost always

Table 3.2
Frequency of Comment Types by School Librarian

Tape Number	General	Somewhat Specific	Specific
1	8	4	2
2	10	6	6
3	15	10	15
4	20	20	20

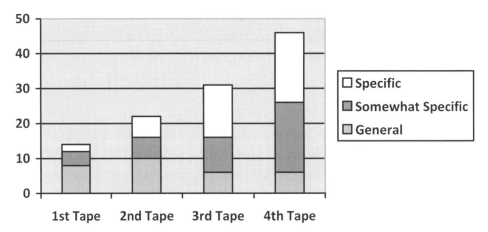

Figure 3.1: School librarian comments.

1. **Group into categories (Table 3.2)**
2. **Charts or graphs (Figure 3.1)**

C. **Interviews and Questionnaires**

1. **Closed questions**
   The results from the two ClassMaps Surveys are given here, first in a table, and then as a bar graph. There is a separate bar graph for each question (see Table 3.3 and Figures 3.2–3.7).

2. **Open questions**
   Because the ClassMaps Survey used in this project does not allow students to make general comments, open questions were not used in this situation.

VI. **What does this tell me about my original question?**

Listening to and coding the comments made to students on the audiotapes shows two things: I did make more specific comments to help students over the course of the experiment, and I made more comments overall by the time I recorded the fourth tape as compared to the first tape.

Also, in examining the table and the charts based on the ClassMaps Survey, the students have shown an increase in their perceptions of their own abilities in terms of the school library.

Table 3.3
Results of Student Responses to Academic Efficacy

	Never		Sometimes		Often		Almost Always	
Question	1st	2nd	1st	2nd	1st	2nd	1st	2nd
1. I know how to use this school library.	20	10	20	10	10	20	10	20
2. I can do as well as most kids in this school library.	18	6	18	22	15	20	9	12
3. I can help others understand how to use the school library.	22	4	22	25	11	20	5	11
4. I can be a very good student in this school library.	20	10	20	20	10	15	10	15
5. I can do the hard work in this school library.	16	11	23	12	11	22	10	15
6. I expect to do very well when I work hard in this school library	16	11	23	12	11	22	10	15

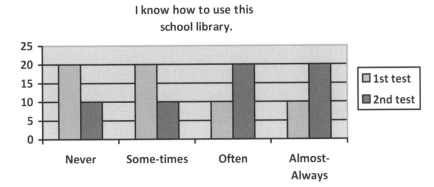

Figure 3.2: Student responses to ClassMap Survey questions.

VII. Using the information

A. How does this help me make decisions or better understand resilience in my school library?

Based on the numbers and figures above there seems to be some improvement. Based on my observations and interactions with the students, they do appear to be more comfortable and confident in the school library.

B. Use the information to decide whether to continue the current activity, make changes to the current activity, or devise and implement another activity.

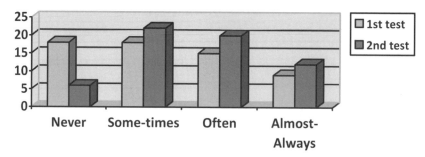

Figure 3.3: Student responses to ClassMap Survey questions.

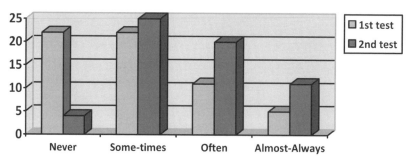

Figure 3.4: Student responses to ClassMaps questions.

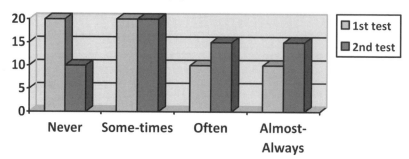

Figure 3.5: Student responses to ClassMap Survey questions.

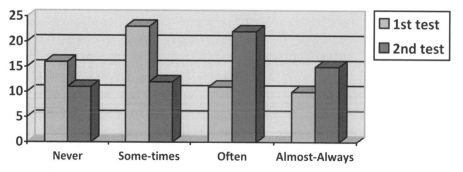

Figure 3.6: Student responses to ClassMap Survey questions.

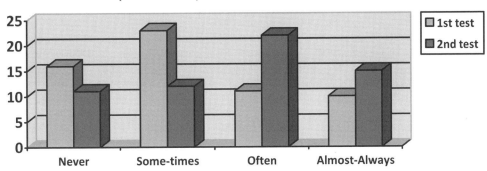

Figure 3.7: Student responses to ClassMap Survey questions.

This is the first year I have tried to teach the second graders to use the OPAC, even though this was limited to simple searches. I believe it has been a success, and I will continue to do this with other classes. Also, the use of the tape recorder has helped me to be more aware of the way I give guidance to students using the library. This will help me be a more effective teacher.

C. Share the information with students, teachers, and administrators.

I will put a brief summary in my report to the principal and bring it up at the next faculty meeting, if appropriate.

REFERENCES

Bandura, A. (1969). *Principles of behavior modification*. New York: Holt, Rinehart and Winston.

Bandura, A. (1993). Perceived self-efficacy in cognitive development and functioning. *Educational Psychologist, 28*(2), 117–148.

Bandura, A. (1997). *Self-efficacy: The exercise of control*. New York: W. H. Freeman.

Eisenberg, M., & Berkowitz, R. (1990). *Information problem-solving: The big 6 skills approach to library and information skills instruction*. Norwood, NJ: Ablex.

Kuhlthau, C. C. (1993). *Seeking meaning: A process approach to library and information service*. Norwood, NJ: Ablex.

Pajares, F. (1996). Self-efficacy beliefs in academic settings. *Review of Educational Research, 66*, 543–578.

Ridley, D. S., & Walther, B. (1995). *Creating responsible learners: The role of a positive classroom environment*. Washington, DC: American Psychological Association.

Schunk, D. H., & Pajares, F. (2005). Competence perceptions and academic functioning. In A. J. Elliot & C. S. Dweck (Eds.), *Handbook of competence and motivation* (pp. 85–104). New York: Guilford Press.

Seifert, T. L., & Wheeler, P. (1994). Enhancing motivation: A classroom application of self-instruction strategy training. *Research in Education, 51*, 1–10—.

Urdan, T., & Turner, J.C. (2005). Competence motivation in the classrooms. In A.J. Elliot & C.S. Dweck (Eds.), *Handbook of competence and motivation* (pp. 297–317). New York: Guilford Press.

Zimmerman, B.J., & Kitsantas, A. (2005). The hidden dimension of personal competence: Self-regulated learning and practice. In A.J. Elliot & C.S. Dweck (Eds.), *Handbook of competence and motivation* (pp. 509–526). New York: Guilford Press.

4

Self-Selected Learning Goals

According to Seifert and Wheeler (1994), one of the three most important findings from contemporary psychological research is that "students must believe they are responsible for their learning" (p. 6). Ultimately, a purpose of schooling is that students will become self-directed adults who are able to take charge of their own learning and master the skills and knowledge that they need to meet their career and personal goals. This skill is critically important in a society that values "life long learners." More immediately, students are expected to become gradually more independent as they move through successive grades, and so their school success depends in part on their ability to apply themselves to a specific task without constant adult input and supervision. As Zimmerman and Kitsantas (2005) note, "there is growing evidence that students who use self-regulatory processes frequently enjoy greater success and are more motivated" (p. 510).

Self-directed learning requires that students have a strong sense of academic efficacy (discussed in Chapter 3) and that they are facile at monitoring and controlling their moment-to-moment behaviors (discussed in Chapter 5). However, this chapter focuses very specifically on the core self-regulatory processes that students need to take charge of their own learning: goal setting, analyzing tasks and determining appropriate strategies to accomplish them, time management, observing and tracking their performance, judging the quality of their work, identifying and locating the proper environment, and knowing when to seek help (Zimmerman & Kitsantas, 2005).

The heart of self-directed learning is students' capacity to hold personal goals for their own learning. These goals provide focus to the students' learning by providing a "target" that they can visualize, and toward which they can direct their efforts, and by directing them away from goal-irrelevant activities (Locke & Latham, 2002). Subsequent choices about what they should learn or how to learn are easier once they have been framed within a targeted goal. For example, if the students' learning goal is to understand the advantages and disadvantages of bankruptcy for consumers, it will be important for them to know more about credit ratings, but it might not be important to understand how the stock market sets the value of stocks. Goals also contribute to students' persistence when learning because they define the end point of a learning task— until the students understand bankruptcy's advantages as well as the disadvantages, they know that they should continue seeking more information. In a similar way, goals also prompt students to extend and expand their efforts when this flexibility is instrumental in helping them reach their goal. For example, the students' original intention might be to search the Internet for more information about bankruptcy. However, they might decide that it would clarify their understanding to visit with a banker or interview a bankruptcy attorney. Thus, learning goals prompt students to take whatever steps are necessary for them to achieve their goal. Learning goals that are personally meaningful for students can energize their learning by reinforcing its personal worth for them and by reminding them that their learning is purposeful and pragmatically useful.

Goal setting is neither easy nor effortless for many students. Instead, students need practice and scaffolded adult support in order to set and work purposely toward personal learning goals (Sands & Doll, 2000). Still, once they receive this support, many students' capacities for goal setting surpass the expectations of their teachers and other adults. Their facility with goal setting can be broken down into five specific steps:

1. Making the goal,
2. Remembering the goal that they have set,
3. Planfully altering their behavior in ways that increase their likelihood of reaching the goal,
4. Judging whether or not they are making progress toward their goal, and
5. Judging whether or not they have met the goal.

Students who are unfamiliar with or unskilled at goal setting will need to be carefully guided through each of these steps.

Goals can be easier or harder to meet, and can have more or less impact on students learning, depending on five key characteristics (Bandura, 1997). First, goals have more impact if they are specific, clear definitions of the purpose of learning so that students can readily tell whether or not they have met the goal. Vague or very general goals are ultimately confusing for students, and they hold very little power over their learning. Second, effective goals are moderately difficult. Goals that are too easy do not prompt students to increase their effort or commitment to learning, while goals that are much too difficult will quickly overwhelm students. Moderately difficult goals, that may even be somewhat higher than adults *think* the students can achieve, are the most motivating (Sands & Doll, 2000). Third, proximal goals describing an achievement that students could expect to accomplish in the next week or month are far more influential than distal goals that might require one or several years to accomplish. To some extent, the proximity of an effective goal is age-related: students in the early elementary grades can be helped to work toward goals that are one week away; late elementary–aged students can work toward goals of up to a month away with assistance; middle school students might be able to work toward goals for a two-month grading period; and early high school students can usually work toward goals for an academic semester. All of these timelines can shift once students have more practice and experience with goal setting. Fourth, goals can be set by the students themselves (also called intrinsic or internal goals) or might instead be given to students by the teacher or school librarian (also called extrinsic or external goals). Intuitively, it seems that self-set goals would naturally be more motivating for students, but there is some evidence that adult-set goals can be equally powerful as long as students can relate the goals to purposes meaningful for their own lives. Fifth, learning goals can be *mastery goals* that describe a purpose of mastering a skill or information, or they can be *competitive goals* that describe a purpose of performing better than other students (Pintrich & Schunk, 1996). Mastery goals are more effective in motivating student effort and learning because they describe an outcome that is under the students' control, while competitive goals depend, in part, on the performance of other students and so are less predictable and less effective. Optimal goals will be mastery goals that are specific, moderately difficult, for an age-appropriate interval of time, and meaningful to the students.

Learning strategies play a critical role in fostering students' autonomy in learning. Self-directed learners know a variety of learning strategies, can select the best strategy to use for a particular task, are skilled at using the strategy, and will spontaneously use strategies that advance their learning without prompts or instructions from adults (Paris, Byrnes, & Paris, 2001). Younger students or less successful students are less strategic in their learning because they are only familiar with a very few learning strategies and are not as ready to figure out the right strategy to use. More importantly, even if they are told which strategy to use and how to use it, less successful learners will not use the strategy unless an adult reminds them to do so. Consequently, an important role of the school librarian is directly teaching students a variety of literacy and information-seeking strategies and prompting them to use these strategies correctly until the students become independently strategic.

Self-regulated learners will have "a broad repertoire of study strategies, the self-regulatory capacity to apply and refine the strategies on their own, and the sense of self efficacy to accept academic work as a personal challenge" (Zimmerman, Bonner, & Kovach, 1996, p. 137).

Self-directed learning includes goal setting within a larger set of seven skills that foster students' abilities to work independently (Zimmerman & Kitsantas, 2005). These seven skills are:

1. **Goal setting.** If students can look at an assignment or activity and identify what they want to accomplish, they are setting a goal for that activity or assignment.
2. **Analyzing tasks and determining appropriate strategies to accomplish them.** As teachers and school librarians plan instruction, it is important that they help students break tasks down into discrete steps that can be used to successfully complete the assignment or activity. For example, if students need to find information on the agricultural products of a country, they need to first write down what they need to know, go to the OPAC or Internet to look up information on that country, evaluate the sources located to see if they might have the information needed, and then either go to that source and look for the information or return to and refine the search if the first try was not successful. These steps should be repeated until the correct information has been found.
3. **Time management.** Students need to learn how to budget the time they have available to work on an activity or assignment. Some students will

spend 90 percent of their time on the initial part of the assignment, and others realistically manage their time to ensure they can finish all segments of the assignment. It is useful to discuss time management with students to help them recognize when to move on to the next step. For example, when working on a major research paper, high school students may not be able to determine when it is time to quit looking for information and begin writing the paper. It can help these students if the teacher and school librarian work with them to construct a reasonable timeline for the assignment. For a four-week assignment, students should work to refine their problem statement in the first week, then spend two weeks researching and digging for information, and spend the last week writing the final paper (two days for a rough draft, two days to review the draft, then two days to polish a final draft).

4. **Observing and tracking task performance.** Students do not automatically know how to keep track of their work and the steps they need to go through to finish an activity or assignment. One technique that can help is to create a checklist of steps for students to follow. Checking off the steps completed in the correct order can help students see what they have already accomplished and what they still need to do. As students become more accomplished in their skills, they may no longer need the checklist or may be able to write their own while other students could prefer to keep using the adults' checklist.

5. **Judging the quality of their work.** Sometimes it is hard for students to realistically evaluate the quality of their work. Some students believe they have done very well when, in fact, they have not done the assignment correctly. Others notice a large number of errors in their work when, in fact, they have completed a nice piece of work. One of the big advantages of rubrics for assignments and activities is that they help students accurately evaluate the quality of their work. Rubrics can be one of the most effective ways to help students learn to critically judge their own work. At first, some students may need individual guidance in using the rubric to review their work.

6. **Identifying and locating the proper environment.** Some students need absolute quiet when reading, studying, or writing. Others cannot function in complete quiet and need a location with a steady level of background noise. Some students tolerate visual distractions, while others have a very high tolerance for noise. It is important for students to be aware of the conditions that are most conducive for them to work and study. The school librarian and teacher should help students identify their own work and study styles, and then make it possible for students to find and work in their most comfortable environment. The school library should provide quiet study areas and places for quiet interaction.

7. **Know when to seek help.** Every student needs help sometimes. Students need to learn to recognize situations when they need help and identify individuals whom they can ask for help. It can be appropriate for students to ask the school librarian, teachers, other adults, or fellow students when they

need assistance, and the environment in the school library and the classroom should support students seeking help.

SUGGESTIONS

School librarians at all levels should help students learn, apply, and practice skills for self-directed learning. These include goal setting skills, as well as skills in monitoring their performance, applying appropriate strategies, and managing their work settings. There are several alternative ways that this support can be made available to students: modeling the skills so that students can observe their performance, direct questioning that prompts students to self-reflect on their performance, or providing rubrics so that students can systematically evaluate their performance. In addition, the instructional strategies that support students' development of academic efficacy (Chapter 3) and of behavioral self-control (Chapter 5) will be similarly useful in promoting students' independent learning.

Modeling

Students can learn by observing what other people are doing. Thus, when planning instruction, it is important to show or model the sequence of steps that students can follow to successfully complete the assignment. For example, when teaching second graders how to use guide words in a dictionary, use several examples with strong visual aids to help students understand the process. Eventually, students will be able to successfully use guide words independently.

Questioning

Self-directed learning is also strengthened by asking students to explain or talk aloud about what they are doing as they work on an activity or an assignment. For example, students may be asked, "What do you want to do today? How do you intend to do it?" This technique can help students learn to stop and think about what they are doing, pay attention to their strategies and whether these are helpful, or plan an effective approach before starting to work. This can lay the foundation for success.

Rubrics

Construct a rubric whenever giving students an assignment or activity, and review this rubric with students when the assignment is given, not after it has been evaluated. The rubric will ensure that the assignment matches the goals and objectives of the lesson and will help ensure fair, consistent grading. More importantly, students can use the rubric to make sure they understand what they need to do and to self-evaluate the quality of their work. The benefits of rubrics make the work needed to construct them worthwhile, and grading will be easier.

PLANNING FOR RESILIENCE

It is important to determine the effectiveness of efforts to teach students to be self-directed learners. The following example focuses on rubrics and uses the research template discussed in Chapter 3 and included in the appendix.

HOW CAN I FIND OUT?

I. **Scenario** (Here I describe the situation that is the issue; that I am worried about, etc.)

In my middle school, students do not seem to have realistic grade expectations. Too often, they believe they have received a lower grade on assignments than they deserve. I have worked with a seventh grade teacher to teach students to create a simple PowerPoint presentation as part of their American Revolution reports. I tried using rubrics with students to help them learn how to evaluate the quality of their own work.

II. **Resilience Area and Activities**(Here I decide which area of resilience to focus on and how to do that.)

Resilience area: Self-selected learning goals

I used a rubric as a tool to help students understand how they will be evaluated and to provide guidance for self-evaluation.

III. **Question** (What is the main question I need to answer to decide whether or not the technique I chose is enhancing resilience?)

Do students who are provided rubrics evaluate the quality of their work more realistically than students doing assignments without rubrics?

IV. **Methodology** (How will I gather information to answer the question?)

A. **What information do I need to gather?**

Because I am interested in whether or not rubrics made a difference in the accuracy of student evaluations of their own work, I need to compare the expectations of students who have been given rubrics with the expectations of students who have not been given rubrics.

B. **How might I gather that information?**

1. Use **existing records** or information.
   There is no information available at this time that specifically addresses the grades that students expect to receive.

2. **Observe** what is happening
   I need information on student beliefs, so observation will not be effective.

3. **Gather information** from people directly.

   a. **Interview**
   An interview would not be appropriate in this case for two reasons: some students may be reluctant to tell me what grade they believe they have earned, and it would take a lot of time to talk to all students.

   b. **Questionnaire**
   A brief question will be included as part of the assignment asking students to indicate how many points they believe they have earned on this assignment.

c. **Test**

While this could be one assessment to use to have students evaluate their performance, it can be a very tense situation for students who are anxious about testing. So, I will not use this.

d. **Assignment or Exercise**

A rubric will be designed for the assignment on creating a PowerPoint. This rubric will be reviewed with two classes of students before they begin the assignment. One part of the assignment will ask students to self-evaluate themselves using a copy of the rubric, which they will turn in with their assignment. The other two classes will also be asked to self-evaluate, but they will not have access to the rubric until after the assignment is completed.

C. **Collect the data** (using the technique identified in Section B).

I am working with the social studies teacher who has four classes of seventh graders who will all do the same assignment. We will have students in two classes self-evaluate their work using the rubric. The other students will be asked to indicate the number of points they believe they will earn on the assignment but will not have access to the rubric. The rubric that will be used is given here.

Seventh Grade American Revolution Assignment: Power Point Rubric

Topic	Target (10–9 points)	Acceptable (8–6 points)	Unacceptable (5–0 points)
Mechanics	6 slides Type is easy to read Grammar and spelling correct Layout is easy to follow May use advanced elements such as animation	4–5 slides Type could be larger Two or more mistakes in grammar or spelling Problems with layout	Less than 4 slides Significant problems with type, grammar, spelling, and/or layout
Content	Background and context for the historical event are given. Good discussion questions included. Information is accurate.	Some background and/or context missing. Discussion questions will not promote discussion. Some mistakes in information.	Significant problems in one or more of background, context, questions, or accuracy.
Sources	At least 4 different sources used. Both print and digital resources used. Complete, accurate citations given for all sources used.	Only 2 or 3 sources used. Only print or only digital sources used. Citations incomplete or inaccurate or missing.	Only 1 source used, or; Only print or only digital sources used; and/or Citations missing.

A = 30–25 points; B = 24–20 points; C = 19–15 points; D = 14–10 points; F = < 10 points

V. **Data Analysis** (Now what do I do with all this information?)

A. Numbers

1. **Frequencies**

It is often very useful to create a table of frequencies for data collected. In this case, Table 4.1 compares student self-evaluation grades and the actual grades assigned by the school librarian.

2. **Bar graphs**

Depending on circumstances, it could be useful to create a bar graph.

3. **Percentages**

Sometimes percentages show difference more dramatically or in a way that is easier to understand (see Table 4.2).

4. **Pie graph**

Given the four different sets of percentages, pie graphs cannot convey the information in one graph. Therefore, this would not be useful.

Table 4.1
Student/Librarian Evaluations

	Students with access to rubric		Students without access to rubric	
Grade	Student	Librarian	Student	Librarian
A	15	14	20	12
B	13	13	15	10
C	12	8	5	11
D	0	3	0	4
F	0	2	0	3

Table 4.2
Percentages of Students Receiving Different Grades

	Students with access to rubric		Students without access to rubric	
Grade	Student	Librarian	Student	Librarian
A	37%	35%	50%	30%
B	32%	32%	37%	25%
C	30%	20%	12%	28%
D	0	7%	0	10%
F	0	5%	0	7%

5. **Change over time**

This is not appropriate because the data do not reflect changes over time; instead I am comparing two different groups of students.

B. **Observations**

No observations were done, therefore, I can skip this section.

C. **Interviews and Questionnaires**

No interviews were done; questionnaires were not used. So, I can skip this section also.

VI. **What does this tell me about my original question?**

Examination of the data in Tables 4.1 and 4.2 shows that students who have access to grading rubrics before turning in the assignment can more accurately evaluate their own work. Some students do not do as well as others on self-evaluation even with the rubrics. I will continue to use rubrics, but I will try to identify students who are having trouble developing this skill, and work with them individually.

VII. **Using the information**

A. How does this help me make decisions or better understand resilience in my school library?

I learned that it is possible to work with students to help them understand how to evaluate their own work. I learned also that rubrics are an effective tool to use for this purpose.

B. Use the information to decide whether to continue the current activity, make changes to the current activity, or devise and implement another activity.

I have identified one technique to use to help students learn to accurately self-evaluate their own work. I will continue to develop and use rubrics with students.

C. Share the information with students, teachers, and administrators.

I will share the information with students so they can see the value of learning to accurately evaluate their own work. I will work with teachers (especially in collaboratively designed lessons) to incorporate more rubrics into instructional design and to teach students how to use them. I will report to my principal what I have done and share the results.

REFERENCES

Bandura, A. (1997). *Self-efficacy: The exercise of control.* New York: W. H. Freeman.

Locke, E. A., & Latham, G. P. (2002). Building a practically useful theory of goal setting and task motivation: A 35-year odyssey. *American Psychologist, 57*(9), 705–717.

Paris, S. G., Byrnes, J. P., & Paris, A. H. (2001). Constructing theories, identities, and actions of self-regulated learners. In B. J. Zimmerman & D. H. Schunk (Eds.), *Self-regulated learning and academic achievement: Theoretical perspectives* (pp. 253–287). Mahwah, NJ: Lawrence Erlbaum Associates.

Pintrich, P. R., & Schunk, D. H. (1996). *Motivation in education: Theory, research, and applications.* Englewood Cliffs, NJ: Merrill Prentice-Hall.

Sands, D., & Doll, B. (2000.) *Teaching goal setting and decision making to students with developmental disabilities.* A monograph in the series, Innovations: A research to practice series. Washington, DC: American Association on Mental Retardation.

Seifert, T. L., & Wheeler, P. (1994). Enhancing motivation: A classroom application of self-instruction strategy training. *Research in Education, 51,* 1–10.

Zimmerman, B. J., & Kitsantas, A. (2005). The hidden dimension of personal competence: Self-regulated learning and practice. In A. J. Elliott & C. S. Dweck (Eds.), *Handbook of competence and motivation* (pp. 510–527). New York: Guilford Press.

Zimmerman, B. J., Bonner S., & Kovach, R. (1996). *Developing self-regulated learners: Beyond achievement to self-efficacy.* Washington, DC: American Psychological Association.

5

Behavioral Self-Control

One goal of every educator is well-behaved students. An important capacity of resilient children is the ability to behave appropriately and adaptively with a minimum of adult supervision. This chapter explores research describing school practices that foster students' self-control and suggests strategies that school librarians can use to develop this ability.

The goal of promoting students' self-control differs in important ways from the broader goal of having well-behaved students. There are many adult-centered strategies that are highly effective in squelching students' maladaptive behaviors: commanding students to follow the rules; backing up these commands with incentives for rule-following or negative consequences for rule-breaking; or anticipating and preventing misbehavior by restricting the places where students can go, the things they can do, or the activities they can participate in. Ridley and Walther (1995) identify three disadvantages to these traditional forms of discipline. First, teachers who "police" students often do not have time or rapport to experience the joys of teaching. Second, teachers may stop the misbehavior, but students do not learn how to manage their own behavior. And third, adult-centered discipline is based on the philosophy that punishment will encourage better behavior.

In contrast, student-centered discipline strategies structure settings and situations so that students learn to self-manage their own behavior and, ultimately, to be responsibly independent in their discipline and self-control (Bear, Cavalier, & Cavalier, 2004). In student-centered discipline, students participate in setting the rules, are taught positive and adaptive behaviors to use in lieu of maladaptive and disturbing behaviors, monitor their own behavior to ensure that it follows the rules, and adjust their behavior as necessary so that it is appropriate and furthers their own goals for success in school. As noted by Young, West, Li, and Peterson (1997, p. 90), "Taking responsibility for one's own behavior is a beneficial, lifelong skill and an important teaching objective."

Both student-centered and adult-centered strategies for managing student behavior need to be shaped within the context of the school's program for student discipline. At the very least, it is important for school librarians to adhere to school-wide rules about discipline and student behavior. In addition, instead of individual or classroom-focused plans to teach and encourage student self-control and self-management, Ridley and Walther (1995) describe a whole-school, student-centered discipline plan implemented at a middle school to encourage lifelong learners. In a situation where the whole school chooses to become involved, this plan is very useful.

Still, Bear et al. (2004) point out that student-centered discipline strategies, while highly effective for the majority of students, tend to be ineffective with a small group of students with very disruptive and disturbing behaviors. Particularly challenging students require consistent, adult-managed behavioral supervision that is constant, immediate, and uniform across all classrooms and settings in the school. Thus, the complex task for school librarians is to promote the self-control of the majority of students while simultaneously stepping in to more directly manage the behavior of these few, very challenging students. Consequently, this chapter first describes the essential elements of adult-managed discipline and then provides an extended discussion of strategies to promote students' self-control.

ADULT-MANAGED BEHAVIOR CONTROL

The core of adult-managed discipline programs lies in the essential relationship that exists between the school librarian and the students in a class or school. (See chapter 6 for a more complete discussion about the relationships between students and school librarians.) Students are far more responsive to and cooperative with behavior management programs when these are delivered by adults whose relationships with students are caring, respectful of students' autonomy, and minimize adult–student conflicts. With behaviorally challenging students, it may seem as if the need to form a high-quality relationship works at cross purposes with the need to set and enforce high standards for student behavior. In practice, these are two highly compatible goals.

The building block of any relationship is time—time spent having fun together. This fundamental principle simplifies the task of forging strong relationships with all students who enter the school library. Steal a few moments out of the busy routines of the center to make gentle eye contact with each student. Check in, however briefly, about a grandmother who is ill, a litter of new puppies, or an anticipated trip to visit an older brother. Call students by name. (Use a digital camera to take a photo of each student with a name tag, and review them like flash cards to help memorize names.) Tell a joke or two, perhaps just before the bell rings and the period is over. And find simple ways to praise every student for something that they have done carefully, with great effort, and well. Each of these strategies forges a caring link between adults and students and provides a foundation that prompts students to care about and want to please the school librarian.

Rules

A second very important element of behavioral control is the development and posting of *rules* that will govern students' behavior while they are in the school library. In addition, in adult-managed behavior, information should also be included about what will happen when students do or do not follow the rules. Here is an example of the rules for one elementary school library:

Media Center Rules

1. Step quietly.
2. Speak softly.

3. Share nicely.
4. Start on your work.

Consequences

1. Warning.
2. Separated from group.
3. Conference with your teacher or parents.

Rewards

1. Praise.
2. Treats/Grab Bag.
3. Media Helper. (Used with permission from Patrinia Gilliam, Larchmont Elementary School, Norfolk, VA.)

Once the rules are developed and posted it is important to follow them consistently and equitably for every student in the school.

Observation is one way to document the effectiveness of the posted rules. A checklist can be developed in advance from the list of rules, and then it is relatively simple to quickly note the number of incidences of student misbehavior in the library at a given time or on a given day. There should also be a place to record the number and type of consequences and rewards given. Comparison of the data from the beginning of school to data from the end of school would indicate the effectiveness of the rules and systems of consequences and rewards.

Positive Consequences or Rewards

Teddy Bear

Some elementary school libraries use rewards as consequences of positive student behavior on a regular basis. Such tactics can be effective if the reward is attractive enough to the children. For example, the school library may have a teddy bear who takes turns sitting with children who have been good. The school librarian explains how students can earn their own turn with the bear and why a specific child will have the bear. It is also important to make sure that all children in the class have an opportunity to sit with the teddy bear at least once. For example, at the end of story hour, the school librarian might say, "Danny has listened very well today. Next week, Teddy will sit with him for story time." Other school libraries use a special chair or a seat close to the storyteller, or other reward to encourage good behavior. For older students, an opportunity to be the special helper in the school library may be similarly rewarding. In both examples, it is important to record which child is rewarded when, and also to ensure that all children have a turn. Classwide rewards can be alternatives to selecting a single student for special privilege. For example, a class could earn ping pong balls dropped into a jar, or colored squares pasted onto a chart for good school library behavior, and when the chart or jar is full, the class could earn a special story or might be featured on the school library bulletin board mounted in the hallway. Rules can be formatted into a checklist for recording instances and types of misbehavior and good behavior immediately after the period. These data can be used to evaluate the effectiveness of the reward system.

Tokens

When working with students in the school library, it is very important to leave the front of the class or move from behind the circulation desk and actually move among the students when not actively teaching or reading a story. This close proximity to the students is one way to subtly control their behavior. Also, when correcting a student, it is much better to do so in as private a manner as possible, instead of shouting from the front of the class. One technique that can be helpful is to give students tokens when they are "caught" following the rules. When students misbehave, tokens can be pointedly given to the students nearby who are behaving well. At the end of the period, the tokens can be redeemed for stickers or bookmarks or other similar rewards; and all tokens for a class can be collected in a jar toward a classwide reward. This technique works best if the school librarian is moving among the students instead of remaining at the front of the class. The number of tokens earned can be one way to collect data on the effectiveness of this type of program.

At the same time, it is important to help students learn from their own misbehavior and help them consider alternative behaviors for the future. For example, a simple "think sheet" could be very useful in this type of situation. Students would respond to the following prompts:

- I did _____
- I should have done _____
- Next time I will _____

This exercise gives students the opportunity to accept responsibility for their own behavior and identify appropriate responses for future situations.

Occasional Negative Consequences

Some of the consequences listed with the example of school library rules were punishments—negative consequences that are intended to discourage students from breaking the rules. Punishment is usually a strategy of last resort when building a program of behavior management because even though it is usually effective, it frequently has unintended consequences that can make behavior management even more difficult. The difficulty with punishing consequences is that these leave students resentful or even angry, ultimately affecting their experiences in the school library. Adept use of negative consequences will follow the rule of the $10 tickets: If you knew that every time you were driving one mile over the speed limit on the freeway, you would receive a $10 speeding ticket, chances are that you would never speed. That is not what typically happens, though. Instead, adults receive speeding tickets once or twice for hundreds of instances of speeding and when they are ticketed, the fine is over $100. As a result, people are very often angry at the officer ("There were six other cars going faster that he could have ticketed.") or complain about the speed limits ("They just lowered the speed limit there as a speed trap."). The same pattern will hold in school libraries if students perceive the negative consequences to be unpredictable or very large.

Classroom Meetings

Even when adults are managing the behavior in the school library, it can be useful to gather the students into a classwide meeting to discuss the school library rules. In a classwide meeting, the students work together to answer questions, discuss problems and successes, give their opinions about the school library and its routines, and contribute to decisions about what to do in the future (Developmental Studies Center, 1996). This gives the school librarian a chance to examine the rules with the students, to make sure that everyone is aware of the rules, and to explore reasons for each rule. For example, a school librarian might explain the center rules to students, and then ask which rules are hardest to remember and what could be done to make the rules easier to follow.

Some classes are less familiar with classwide meetings and need to be coached on appropriate ways to participate. For example, establish ground rules so that one person talks at a time and everyone else is listening, make sure every student understands how to take a turn talking, and guide the discussion so that it stays on topic. Often, a chart tablet at the front of the meeting can focus the discussion. Write the question in bold letters at the top of the page, and then list student ideas and opinions as they contribute them. In some cases, the meeting can be closed with a vote by students to select their top three recommendations or ideas (Developmental Studies Center, 1996). While students' time in the school library is more limited than in the classroom, the school librarian works with students for their entire enrollment in the school instead of for one grade or one class.

PROMOTION OF STUDENTS' SELF-CONTROL

Self-control differs from adult-managed behavior in that the student takes responsibility for monitoring their own behavior and directing it to be consistent with adult expectations. Developmental researchers have identified the capacity for self-control as one of the important abilities that children acquire with age and experience, and they have proposed several alternative explanations for its emergence. Six conceptual frameworks for shaping students' self control are discussed here, together with their implications for school practices.

Internalized Speech

A fundamental theory, Vygotsky's (1962) internalized speech, suggests that very young children first learn to alter their behavior in response to spoken commands of their parents or other caretakers. Over time, they take on the adult's role in similar situations, softly speaking the commands to themselves and then following them. Ultimately, they internalize the commands, thinking the words instead of speaking them out loud, while the commands continue to govern their behavior. Self-control emerges at the point where children not only mimic the commands that adults have given to them, but frame their own internalized commands that shape their behavior so that it is consistent with their personal behavioral goals. Within this conceptual framework, one way to promote students' self-control is to directly instruct them in commands that they can use to shape their own behavior in common situations that they encounter in the school library. For example, a student is frustrated when a treasured book is missing from the shelves. Although his first inclination might be to complain in a loud voice, he reminds himself of the rule—"School library voices are quiet voices"—and so stops himself from calling out.

Interpersonal Cognitive Problem Solving

A second useful framework for understanding students' self control is Shure's (2001) interpersonal cognitive problem solving. Children as young as three and four years of age have been taught to solve challenging social problems using four commonsense steps: (1) identify the problem, (2) list multiple alternative solutions, (3) systematically evaluate the solutions and pick the best one, and (4) try it and evaluate how well it works (Spivack & Shure, 1974). The social problem-solving framework for self-control is easily applied within school libraries. For example, if one student has some materials overdue and another student is waiting to check them out, the students might (separately or together) be asked to list several possible steps that they could take to solve the problem, carefully think about the advantages and disadvantages of each step, then choose one and try it out. Initially, this could take more time than simply giving the students instructions about what to do, but over time, students' self-directed problem solving will be more responsible and more efficient.

A special case of social problem solving has frequently been used to help impulsive students to learn to be more reflective and careful in their behavior (Bash & Camp, 1985; Kendall & Braswell, 1993). The special problem of impulsive children is that they tend to act first, without thinking, and then will realize after the fact that their behavior was maladaptive and likely to result in negative consequences. To foster their self-regulation, an additional first step is integrated into the problem-solving procedures—"Stop and think." Stopping interrupts the students' automatic tendency to respond to minor frustrations in ways that are aggressive, loud, or thoughtless. Then, once they have stopped, students are guided into the problem-solving steps: What is the problem? What are my choices? Pick one. How does it work? First, students are instructed in the steps and rehearse them repeatedly with different examples. Then, the steps are posted at key points around the school library. When difficult situations arise, adults can cue them that this is a situation when the problem-solving strategies would be helpful. For example, "Hidalgo, remember the stop and think steps that we learned last week. Talk through them with me." Soon, brief and subtle reminders will be enough to cue the students. "Liam, what are your steps?"

Teaching Effective Routines

In some cases, students can be taught simple routines to counteract many of the likely behavior problems that might arise in the school library. For example, in most schools the school library will have routines for places to sit when the class comes to the library, checking in when coming on a pass from study hall, how to ask for help, or how to share the computers available for student use. Direct instructional strategies can be used to teach these routines to students (Witt, LaFleur, Gilbertson, & Naquin, 1999). First, the routine needs to be described in a series of steps. For example, the steps for "entering the school library at the beginning of a class" might be:

1. Walk quietly down the hall with the classroom teacher.
2. Make a line along the blue wall, right outside the school library.
3. The first student in the line should open the door to the school library and look at the face of the school librarian.
4. When the school librarian nods, the student should hold the door open for the rest of the class.
5. Each student in the class should walk quietly into the school library and sit on the red rug in the corner.

Next, this routine is modeled for the students. For example, two or three students from an older grade might demonstrate for first grade students how to enter the school library. Then, the routine is systematically practiced by the students—the first graders would walk through entering the school library, four or five times in a row. After each time, the school librarian should hold up a chart that lists all five steps and put a check next to those steps that the students completed correctly. This feedback prompts students to remember the steps and reinforces their good work in following the steps that they performed. Periodically, over the next several weeks, students can be reminded of the routine with a check-back session in which the school librarian again rates their "entering" performance using the list of steps and praises their good behavior. If the class begins to slip back into their former, noisy entering behaviors, one or two booster sessions of repracticing the steps is usually sufficient to reestablish the routine.

Self-Modification

The fourth framework for understanding self-control can be found within the applied behavior analysis focus on antecedents and contingencies of target behaviors. This ABC (antecedents, behaviors, consequences) framework for behavioral control underlies much of the classroom management strategies that are used in school classrooms. When used as adult-centered discipline strategies, teachers typically impose negative consequences on problem behaviors to reduce their occurrence, and they use positive consequences to reward and increase the occurrence of positive behaviors. Antecedents are sometimes manipulated as well, when teachers alter situations that appear to prompt misbehavior. For example, students who frequently erupt in anger when classmates squeeze by their desk to sharpen their pencils might be moved to a desk located far from the pencil sharpener.

ABC frameworks can also be the basis of students' self-control when antecedents and consequences are manipulated by *students* themselves instead of by adults (Shapiro, Durnan, Post, & Levinson, 2002). In self-modification programs, students can participate in setting goals for their own behavior, self-monitoring their positive behaviors or disturbing behaviors, imposing their own consequences in response to these observations, and evaluating how well their self-modification program is working.

Self-monitoring is composed of two elements: "(a) *observation* of one's own behavior, and (b) *recording* that behavior in some way" (Shapiro et al., 2002, p. 433). Evidence indicates that self-monitoring can be used with any and all students, and with a wide variety of target behaviors. Then, seven steps are recommended:

1. Define the target behavior in clear and simple terms, and work carefully to identify various types of appropriate and inappropriate behavior. Then state these in ways that make sense to the students. For example, talking to your study partner while the teacher or school librarian is teaching is inappropriate; discussing the assignment with your study partner(s) during work time is appropriate; working on assigned activities is appropriate; goofing off—even quietly—is not.
2. Design a method to record behavior. This must match the desired behavior and must be easy for the student to understand and use. For example, a paper could have four columns for check marks: one for talking inappropriately, one for talking appropriately, one for working quietly on task, and one for goofing off.
3. Design a prompt to indicate when it is time to record behavior. This prompt could be a timer or alarm clock, a beep on a tape recorder, or a teacher comment or gesture. Whether the whole class or only specific students are involved in recording behavior will help determine whether a verbal or nonverbal (e.g., tap on the shoulder) cue should be used.
4. The method devised for the student to record his/her behavior should be portable, available, and unobtrusive but obvious and easy to use. Most classrooms use paper and pencil devices.
5. It is important to decide when and how often students will record their behavior—all of the time every time they come to the school library, or only every other week? The type of behavior being monitored and the specific students involved will help determine which method is most effective.
6. An important element of this technique is to check the accuracy of the student records. One way to do this is to compare adult records with those of the students. The teacher, the school librarian, or a library clerk should keep records to compare with the student's self-recordings. Preparation of a special sheet with all student names and all types of behavior will facilitate the recording process. If the disparity is too great (e.g., only 50% agreement), it may be necessary to discuss the procedures for self-monitoring further with the students.
7. It is important to teach the students how to fill out the self-recording sheets. For some students and classes, verbal instructions may be sufficient. Other students may need modeling or role playing.

One key element of self-monitoring is that it helps students to focus on their own actions and become more aware of how they are behaving at a given time. As a result of becoming more aware of their behavior, they may become more adept at controlling themselves. Self-monitoring has the advantage of a build-in data collection system. The self-recording sheets provide specific details about the behavior of specific students and for the class as a whole. These data can be used to determine whether students are behaving more appropriately under this system than they were before it was implemented.

Simplified Self-Monitoring

The self-monitoring system described previously is quite involved and may not be practical in all school libraries. Young and his colleagues (1997) suggest a similar model that combines self-monitoring and self-evaluation with reinforcement. First, it is important to discuss the school library rules with the students. Then devise a rating system to evaluate student behavior. For example,

- 1 = "I did a great job!" The student paid attention, focused on assigned work and/or activities, did not talk inappropriately, contributed to discussion appropriately, and could not have been a better citizen in the school library.

- 2 = "Sometimes I did well, and sometimes I didn't." The student mostly paid attention, focused on assigned work and/or activities most of the time, occasionally talked inappropriately, contributed to discussion appropriately, but one or two elements of his/her behavior could be improved.

- 3 = "I didn't follow the rules." The student may not have paid attention, may not have focused on assigned work and/or activities, may have talked inappropriately, and/or several elements of his/her behavior could be improved.

Then, at the end of each class or time in the school library, students turn in a slip of paper with their names on which they have briefly rated their behavior on the given scale of 1 to 3. Students could also write one sentence about one thing done wrong (if a rating of 2 or 3 was noted) and one thing done right (for a rating of 1). The purpose of the self-rating form is to help students learn to be aware of and evaluate their own behavior. It is important to review these slips shortly after the students leave in order to evaluate their accuracy and identify students who may need more work on how to accurately self-evaluate themselves. As the students become better at self-evaluation, their behavior can also improve. Based on point totals over time, students may earn a reward (such as a sticker or bookmark). As noted previously, there is an automatic system for data gathering here, based on the slips the students turn in each time.

Reciprocal Peer Tutoring

Research on self-modification strategies showed that they were sometimes not implemented because they required too much teacher time. Fantuzzo and Rohrbeck (1992) present Reciprocal Peer Tutoring (RPT) as a strategy for both student learning and student self-management. Fourth and fifth grade students were paired to study math, with some groups receiving group rewards. Results indicated peer tutoring with an integrated reward structure helped students become more focused on work with fewer instances of misbehavior. In the school library, this approach could be used after initial instruction. For example, when teaching middle school students to create Power-Point slides, the school librarian could briefly demonstrate and provide students with a handout with step-by-step instructions. Then pairs of students (matched to be approximately equal in ability) could create a PowerPoint slide with specified content.

First, one student would operate the computer while the other student read the step-by-step instructions; then, roles would be reversed. Working in pairs and being actively involved in learning helps students to stay focused on the task at hand, and the amount of misbehavior decreases.

In every strategy described in this chapter—self-commands, problem-solving steps, instruction in routines, or self-management—students are left with competencies that they can use to manage their own behavior in the future. Just as important, these strategies emphasize students' mastery of the *right* ways to behave, while adult-managed discipline strategies frequently emphasize elimination of problem behaviors. Ultimately, students with self-control will require less adult supervision, and the school librarian will have more time to spend teaching information management skills. Still, not all of these self-control frameworks are appropriate for a given situation, and not all are appropriate for a given school. It is important to know and understand the school's plan for supervising student behavior. Some schools implement school-wide systems of rules to govern student behavior, and the school library must conform to and follow any school-wide systems. At the same time, there may be some additional things that can occur in the school library to help students develop self-control.

Individual Student Behavior Plans

Individual students may need more intensive help learning to control their own behavior. It can be effective to identify the characteristics of the student, the situations that are difficult, and the antecedents to and consequences of the student's misbehavior, and then develop an individual plan specific to that student. For example, one student was a creative thinker and found it difficult to focus in class. However, if he listened to classical music, he was better able to focus and to behave. In this case, allowing the student to listen to an iPod with classical music benefited the student, the class, and the adults working with this student. As another example, a student's misbehavior almost always occurred when she was called on to answer a question or to read out loud. Once the student was only asked questions during private conversations with the school librarian, the problem behavior disappeared.

Sometimes it is helpful to talk with a student to discuss reasons for the misbehavior. Listen to the student's comments, and work to understand the issues from that viewpoint. Then try to suggest alternatives to the disruptive behavior. Instead of shouting and arguing when others don't listen, the students could write down their frustrations, or suggest that everyone have a chance to make a statement, or temporarily leave the group until they are able to participate more calmly. Some students need help practicing this alternative behavior two or three times so that they know exactly what to do when they become upset. This type of discussion can help the student realize there are other alternatives, especially when given the opportunity to participate in identifying alternatives (Hill & Hill, 1990).

In some cases, it can be helpful to work with the student to create a written plan of action. Such a plan should be developed jointly with the student, who should have the opportunity to provide input during the development process. Then, both student and school librarian need to sign the plan. Regular meetings to review the plan, note progress, and incorporate changes should be scheduled, perhaps once a month. In some cases, students may be on an individual behavior plan in other classrooms or settings in the school, and the plan for the school library could piggy back on these other plans.

Even though helping students learn self-control can be challenging, the resulting decrease in student misbehavior benefits all students and enhances resilience in the school library.

PLANNING FOR RESILIENCE

It is important to understand whether or not a procedure implemented in the school library is working. For purposes of this example, the simplified self-monitoring system is used in the following template.

HOW CAN I FIND OUT?

I. **Scenario** (Here I describe the situation that is the issue; that I am worried about, etc.)

I work in a small elementary school with kindergarten through sixth grades, and I am on a fixed schedule in the school library. Last year, some of the fourth grade students began to talk too much and to disrupt other activities in the school library. This year, I have decided to focus on improving student behavior. Rather than singling out a few students, I think it might be more effective to take the whole class approach. Therefore, I instituted a simplified self-monitoring program (described previously) with the fifth graders. I created simple sheets for the students to fill out at the end of each class period in the school library, and I discussed the program with students. They earned rewards by accurately reporting good behavior, and the entire class was working for an ice cream party if everybody improved this year. Every six weeks, I shared the cumulative totals for points in each category with each class.

II. **Resilience Area and Activities** (Here I decide which area of resilience to focus on and how to do that.)

Resilience Area 3: Behavioral Self-Control

The following sheet was designed for student use:

Name _____ Date _____

Today in the school library:

_____ I paid attention, focused on assigned work/activities, & did not talk inappropriately.

_____ I mostly paid attention, focused on assigned work/activities most of the time; contributed to class discussion appropriately; but could do one or two things better.

_____ I did not pay attention; or, did not focus on assigned work/activities; or, talked inappropriately; or, several elements of my behavior could be improved.

Reason(s) I gave myself this rating:

III. **Question** (What is the main question I need to answer to decide whether or not the technique I chose is enhancing resilience?)

Has the emphasis placed on behavior in the school library for fifth graders this year been successful in improving behavior?

IV. **Methodology** (How will I gather information to answer the question?)

I have been collecting, reviewing, and correcting (when necessary) the behavior self-reporting sheets after each class. These records will be used to examine student behavior.

A. **What information do I need to gather?**

The information that is available on the self-reporting behavior sheets.

B. **How might I gather that information?**

1. Use **existing records** or information.

The information I need is on the self-reporting behavior sheets that students have filled out and turned in all year. I have confidence in the accuracy of that information because I reviewed them after each class and corrected any sheets where the students reported incorrectly.

2. **Observe** what is happening.

I have noticed student behavior across the year, however, I did not devise a means to accurately record my observations. Therefore, I have only impressions and no data to support my impressions. I may use some of my observations in reporting, but cannot rely on them to be accurate.

3. **Gather information** from people directly.

a. **Interview**

Students may find it intimidating to talk about their behavior with me, so this is not a good technique for this situation.

b. **Questionnaire**

The data already gathered is a form of a survey or questionnaire. I do not need an additional one.

c. **Test**

Not appropriate in this case.

d. **Assignment or Exercise**

Not appropriate in this case.

C. Collect the data (using the technique I identified previously).

The data have already been collected through the use of the behavioral self-reporting sheets.

V. **Data Analysis** (Now what do I do with all this information?)

A. **Numbers**

The behavioral self-reporting sheets have three levels of behavior, reported as 1, 2, or 3. These data can be compiled as frequencies to give an overall look at the number of students reporting in each category.

1. **Frequencies**

The number of students reporting in each category can be collected by week, month, or semester. I will need to decide based on my knowledge of the students and the school. Probably, cumulating the data by month or by semester will be the most helpful. A sample follows, based on a total of 54 students in three classes.

Total Students in Each Behavioral Category*

Category	1st Semester	2nd Semester
1. Well behaved.	526	600
2. Mostly well behaved.	100	40
3. Behavior problems.	22	8

*Corrected as necessary for accuracy by school librarian.

2. **Bar graphs**

Bar graphs are one way to present the data visually. Figure 5.1 shows a bar graph of the data from the previous table.

As can be seen in the graph, most of the students were well behaved. However, the number of incidences of "mostly well behaved" and "had problems" has decreased in the second semester. At the same time, because this a whole class activity, individual students are not singled out. And all students can benefit by learning to accurately assess their behavior.

3. **Percentages**

Not appropriate for these data.

4. **Pie graph**

The two pie charts in Figures 5.2 and 5.3 provide another way to compare student behavior in the first and the second semesters.

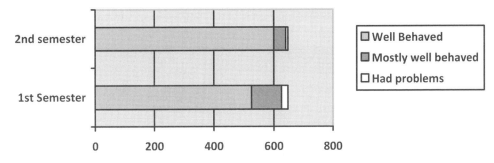

Figure 5.1: Bar graph of self-reported behavior for both semesters.

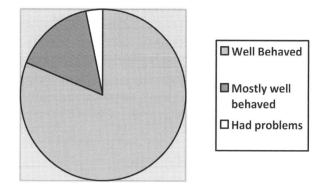

Figure 5.2: Self-reported behavior for the first semester.

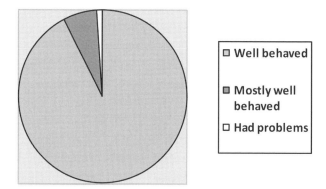

Figure 5.3: Self-reported behavior for the second semester.

As can be seen, this pair of pie graphs provides a different view of the same data as the previous bar graph. Again, examination of the pie graphs shows that there were more "well behaved" cases during the second semester as compared with the first semester. I will need to decide which works best for myself and my educational community.

5. **Change over time**
Because I am interested in the way student behavior has changed over the course of this year, a line graph can be useful. It would look like Figure 5.4.

Examination of the line graph shows that the first two categories (Had problems and Mostly well behaved) were greater in the first semester, and the last category (Well behaved) was greater in the second semester. This would be a positive outcome.

B. **Observations**
Not appropriate in this case since no method was designed to gather the data.

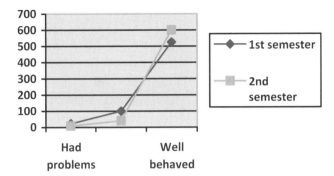

Figure 5.4: Line graph of self-reported behavior for both semesters.

C. Interviews & Questionnaires

Students were not asked to discuss or answer questions about their behavior with me. No separate questionnaire or survey was designed for this project.

VI. What does this tell me about my original question?

The data indicates that student behavior, as reported on the behavioral self-reporting sheets, has improved this year. Further analysis will indicate whether one class or one month was better or worse than others. Overall, the data show improvement in students' ability to behave in the school library. Also, examination of the behavioral self-reporting sheets shows that I had to make corrections in the early ones, but by the middle of the second semester, most reports were accurate.

VII. Using the information.

A. How does this help me make decisions or better understand resilience in my school library?

This technique has helped students be more aware of their behavior, to more accurately report their behavior, and to behave better in the school library than before the use of the behavioral self-reporting sheets.

B. Use the information to decide whether to continue the current activity, make changes to the current activity, or devise and implement another activity.

I will continue to use the behavioral self-reporting sheets with this group of students, although I will only use them once a month instead of weekly. Also, I will use the technique with fifth, fourth, and third graders next year. Overall, the technique takes only a few minutes for each class on a regular basis, and it does support and encourage better behavior. It is beneficial to all students.

C. Share the information with students, teachers, and administrators.

Information on the use of and results from the behavioral self-reporting sheets will be included in my annual report to the principal. Also, as

I collaborate with teachers, I will share with them the technique and my experiences with it. I will also ask the teachers if they have noticed any change in the behavior of the fifth grade students this year.

REFERENCES

Bash, M., & Camp, B. (1985). *Think aloud: Increasing social and cognitive skills—A problem-solving program for children.* Champaign, IL: Research Press.

Bear, G. C., Cavalier, A. R., & Cavalier, M.A.M. (2004). *Developing self discipline and preventing and correcting misbehavior.* Boston, MA: Allyn & Bacon.

Developmental Studies Center. (1996). *Ways we want our class to be: Class meetings that build commitment to kindness and learning.* Oakland, CA: Author.

Fantuzzo, J. W., & Rohrbeck, C. A. (1992). Self-managed groups: Fitting self-management approaches into classroom systems. *School Psychology Review, 21*(2), 255–264.

Hill, S., & Hill, T. (1990). *The collaborative classroom: A guide to co-operative learning.* Portsmouth, NH: Heinemann.

Kendall, P., & Braswell, L. (1993). *Cognitive–behavioral therapy for impulsive children* (2nd ed.). New York: Guilford Press.

Ridley, D. S., & Walther, B. (1995). *Creating responsible learners: The role of a positive classroom environment.* Washington, DC: American Psychological Association,

Shapiro, E. S., Durnan, S. L., Post, E. E., & Levinson, T. S. (2002). Self-monitoring procedures for children and adolescents. In M. R. Shinn, H. M. Walker, & G. Stoner (Eds.), *Interventions for academic and behavior problems II: Preventive and remedial approaches* (pp. 433–441). Bethesda, MD: National Association of School Psychologists.

Shure, M. B. (2001). *I can problem solve: An interpersonal cognitive problem solving program.* Champaign, IL: Research Press.

Spivack, G., & Shure, M. B. (1974). *The problem solving approach to adjustment: A guide to research and intervention.* San Francisco: Jossey-Bass.

Vygotsky, L. S. (1962). *Thought and language.* Cambridge, MA: MIT Press.

Witt, J. C., LaFleur, L., Gilbertson, D., & Naquin, G. (1999). *Teaching effective classroom routines.* Longmont, CO: Sopris West.

Young, K. R., West, R. P., Li, L., & Peterson, L. (1997). Teaching self-management skills to students with learning and behavior problems. *Reclaiming Children and Youth, 6*(2), 90–94.

6

Caring and Authentic Relationships Between Teachers and Students

In the seminal work of developmental resilience researchers, adults' relationships with children emerged as one of the most powerful protective factors predicting the success of vulnerable children (Resnick et al., 1997; Werner, 2006). Subsequently, research on effective schools has verified that adults' relationships with students are a robust predictor of children's educational achievement and their behavioral success (Pianta, 1999; Pianta & Stuhlman, 2004). The single most effective way to make sure that children succeed in school is to be certain that they have ongoing and rich interactions with as many caring adults as possible—adults who respect them, enjoy being with them, expect them to succeed, admire their personal strengths, take responsibility for helping them navigate through troubled times, and celebrate their victories (Doll, LeClair, & Kurien, 2009). In classrooms with high emotional support, "teachers were aware of and responsive to individual students' needs, offered effective and proactive behavior management, and created a positive classroom climate in which teachers and students enjoyed each other and their time in the classroom" (Hamre & Pianta, 2005, p. 962).

An important question is, "How can school librarians make the most of their opportunities to relate to and support their students?" Above all, students need adults to care about them. In very literal terms, this translates into a warm smile, enjoyable delight when the student steps into the school library, a few stolen moments to talk about a new pet or a grandmother's illness, and kind and appreciative words when students learn something new. This kind of caring cannot be counterfeited. It must be genuine and heartfelt, and in addition, it must be communicated carefully and regularly to all students—those who obviously need reassurance as well as those who may not appear to. In a study of middle school students, researchers report, "positive relationships with teachers may serve a particularly important role in facilitating adjustment during early adolescence when youth need nonparental role models and mentors" (Roeser, Midgley, & Urdan, 1996, p. 419).

Caring alone is not enough. A second strand of the most effective adult–student relationships is respect (Walker, 2008; Wentzel, 2002). Respect is obvious when adults expect the most of students, are slow to step in and do something for students that they can do for themselves, and acknowledge students' inner strengths. It is easy to overlook this need for respect when students' hunger for caring is very obvious. For example, teachers in one urban middle school were remarkably warm and invested advocates for their students—but realized that they had been too quick to make excuses for students who failed to complete their work. As one teacher explained, "I know that she lives in an unheated quonset hut, and I'm pretty sure that the family lives without electricity when money gets short. So when she doesn't bring in her homework, I say 'That's ok honey, I know that it was tough to do.' Really, I ought to be saying, 'What can you and I do so that you get your homework done on time?'" The teacher is right—excusing students too quickly sends the unintended message that teachers hold very low expectations for what they can accomplish. Instead, ambitious expectations for every student are empowering, as long as adults help students recognize the small steps they are making toward achieving those goals (positive feedback) without critically dwelling on the ways that their current performance still falls short of excellence (negative feedback.) "High expectations for students was the most consistent positive predictor of students' goals and interest, and negative feedback was the most consistent negative predictor of academic performance and social behavior. Moreover, in contrast to research on parenting, teaching styles appear to explain school-related outcomes for African American as well as European American students" (Wentzel, 2002, p. 299).

A very important foundation of effective adult interactions with students is a consistent and predictable program for managing student behavior. This program must include clear descriptions of how students should behave in the school library and describe the right ways to act instead of listing the prohibited behaviors. Rules should be consistently reinforced in predictable ways by the adults, and mild rather than severe consequences should be used (Bear, Cavalier, & Manning, 2005). When students are involved in creating the rules, are taught strategies for reminding themselves and each other about the rules, participate in keeping simple records of rule-breaking, and impose their own consequences—the school library's behavior management program can become a tool for building students' self-discipline. (See Chapter 5 for more detailed discussion about student behavior.)

Finally, school research has demonstrated a connection between a teacher's instructional excellence and student achievement and behavior. Hamre and Pianta (2005) explain that children who were at risk of school failure in kindergarten benefited from high to moderate levels of instructional support. "High-quality instructional support in this story was observed when teachers made frequent and effective use of literacy instruction, evaluative feedback, instructional conversations and encouragement of child responsibility" (p. 961). In a study with upper elementary grade students, Assor, Kaplan, and Roth (2002) identified the two most effective ways that teachers support student need for autonomy in school work. "These types of behavior are 'fostering relevance' and 'suppressing criticism'" (p. 272).

The bonds that form between teachers and students are often compared to those between students and their parents (Kesner, 2000). Like parents, teachers represent emotional security and a source of values for students (Pianta, 1999). In one study of middle school students, researchers report, "positive relationships with teachers may serve a particularly important role in facilitating adjustment during early adolescence when youth need nonparental role models and mentors" (Roeser et al., 1996, p. 419).

Relationships with teachers are especially important for students' academic success, particularly when students are struggling (Brooks & Goldstein, 2007). In elementary schools, closeness and lack of conflict between teachers and students predict students' academic success (Birch & Ladd, 1997), and the ease with which students transition to new grades or schools (Birch & Ladd, 1998). Strong teacher–student relationships can include those in which teachers clearly and consistently enforce rules. Research with high school physics students has shown that students achieve more when their teachers manage classroom behavior effectively (Brekelmans, Wubbels, & Levy, 1993). Finally, in an analysis of studies designed to identify causes of poor attendance, Epstein and Sheldon (2002) report that "To prevent and correct serious attendance problems, schools need to . . . intensify interpersonal relationships between students and teachers" (p. 309).

SUGGESTIONS

The school librarian is one of the school's professionals who is responsible for creating caring and authentic relationships with students. Working with individual students, small groups of students, or whole classes of students, the school librarian will have many opportunities to demonstrate appreciation for and enjoyment of the students throughout the school day and even during after-school activities.

Based on the research discussed in this chapter, there are some specific things that school librarians can do to help foster positive relationships with their students.

- Instructional support—A school librarian can provide instructional support in many different ways, including guidance on using the OPAC, posters in the school library listing steps to follow to successfully find information in a variety of places, or taking the time to guide students from the OPAC to the shelves to find books they need. Overall, it is important for students to feel comfortable asking questions or seeking help when they need it. School librarians can support this by making students feel their questions are valid and giving students the attention they need when asking for help.

- High emotional support—By providing a welcoming environment, school librarians can help all students feel welcome and accepted for who they are. Take the time to visit with students as often as possible, and learn about what else is happening in their lives. One student proudly came to show his school librarian the new cowboy hat he had bought over the weekend. While his enthusiasm was not school-related, it was important to him and demonstrated the type of strong, supportive, professional bond that can develop between a student and the school librarian. At the same time, be sure to enforce all school library rules fairly and equally. Be sure to stick to the publicized rules and consequences for all students at all times. It is *extremely* important to students that everyone be treated fairly.

- Fostering relevance—It is not unusual for students to wonder why they need to study a particular topic. High school students may ask, "How is Shakespeare going to help me get a job?" Sharing the objectives for a particular lesson or telling students why they need to learn how to conduct an effective Web search can be included in the lessons being taught. This can help students better connect school with the real world.

- Suppressing criticism—As an educator, it is important to correct students when they make mistakes. At the same time, this correction should be done in a supportive, positive way so students learn from their mistakes and are ready to continue trying. Don't just say, "That's wrong." Instead, work with the student to identify what has been done right, and find the place or time when the student began to make mistakes. Then help the student to understand what is wrong and why, and let him/her work to correct the errors.

- High expectations—As the research has consistently shown, if educators expect students to succeed and to produce high-quality work, they are much more likely to do so. A school librarian with a positive attitude about what the students can and should be able to learn and do can enable them to succeed.

- School library atmosphere—While part of the atmosphere is based on the physical facility, the relationship between the school librarian and the students is also very important. It is important for the students to know that the school librarian likes and enjoys them and, at the same time, will fairly and equitably enforce the rules.

What Students Want

Students do not want teachers who are "buddies" and "best friends." They do not want teachers who are extremely permissive. Instead, they want an adult in control who creates a firm, supportive atmosphere. This applies to the school library, also. Comments from students in grades 4 through 12 in focus groups give "real world" examples of what students do want. Among their responses pertaining to teachers:

- "You do better if you know you have someone at school who is cheering you on."

- "The only thing I look for in a teacher is a teacher who respects me. I mean if they respect me and listen, too."

- "Teachers should not judge, but encourage . . . you are afraid to do it because you might get it wrong and people make fun of you."

- "Expect us to do well, but if we make a mistake or get a bad grade, don't yell at us, but at the same time, don't just not care."

- "Being supportive, not all students will be as good as others and you should be supportive of everyone. Recognize everyone's strengths and weaknesses so you support the ones that are not only good or somewhat skilled in the subject, but also the ones that need a little help."

- "Teachers need to make it comfortable to ask for help." (Christenson & Anderson, 2002, p. 385)

Ten Commandments

Karns (1994) offers specific advice and activities for teachers to use to build positive relationships with students. She provides a list of 10 commandments for adults in children's lives than can give everyone some things to think about. By applying these 10 commandments, school librarians can demonstrate their support of students at all levels.

1. *Praise well and often.* Everyone likes to be told they have done something well or that their efforts have been recognized. In one school, a fifth-grade student has Tourette Syndrome, which results in inappropriate vocalizations at times. This student has used the illness as an opportunity to explain the disease to others. One day the school librarian complimented the student's attitude toward the disease and the positive way the student works to explain its manifestations to others. The next day, the student's mother told the school librarian how much she appreciated the support and praise given to the student the day before—and remarked how much it helped the student to know that an adult saw and understood. By taking time to listen to students (at all grade levels), the school librarian can find ample opportunity to compliment them on achievements or activities.

2. *Give children opportunities to control and to choose.* In the school library, this can be as simple as allowing students to check out books of their choice. Or, it is possible to work with students to identify materials they may want in the collection. For example, if students want a particular magazine in the school library, they could circulate a petition. If they get enough signatures, the school librarian could get the magazine, subject to his/her professional judgment. By soliciting student input for collection development, students begin to feel ownership for the school library and understand that their opinions are important.

3. *Look for the positive in all situations.* Disappointments are part of life; however, one's reaction to them can be very influential. The football team might lose the critical game of the season. Instead of complaining about the loss, talk with students about the good plays made during the game and highlight the achievements of individual members of the team throughout the season. In spite of the unfortunate outcome of the last game, many positive things came out of playing football, and students may need help in learning to focus on the positive things.

4. *Be responsible, and give responsibility.* As students get older, they need opportunities to practice becoming more responsible. For example, work with students to help them remember to bring back their overdue books. For younger students, a sticker for each book returned on time may help them to remember. With older students, the school librarian may ask students where the books are. The standard answer is, "I returned it already." One successful response is to make a deal with the students—if they will go home and look in the piano bench, under the car seat, or behind the bed, the school librarian will look in the library. This nonconfrontational approach,

which invites the student to help solve the problem, is often very successful. And, sometimes the book has already been returned to the school library and is found on the shelf or in the back room!

5. *Validate feelings.* All people have times when they feel happy, sad, frustrated, or disappointed. The role of the school librarian, as an adult in student lives, is to understand and help students deal with these feelings. One way is to share personal feelings with students, such as statements like: "When I was in the second grade, I was always afraid to volunteer to give answers in class because I was afraid I would be wrong." In most cases, it is not necessary to discuss all details of a particular incident with the students; just take time to let students know others can understand.

6. *Focus on what it will take to make it right, to make it better, or to make it different.* One of the most frustrating things for students is to feel or to be powerless when it isn't necessary. In some cases, it is possible to work with students to discuss and identify what has caused the concern, and then think about what could be done to correct it. Some things cannot be changed, because they are not under the control of the school librarian. Other things can be addressed. For example, if students are frustrated because all books they need for research are already checked out, discuss with them ways to prevent this in the future. Solutions may include limiting the number of research books that can be checked out by one person, finding appropriate sites on the Web and creating links from the school library home page, borrowing books from the public library, or allowing reference books to go home overnight. It is a good idea to have students help brainstorm alternatives. Then, try to find some good sources for the student to use that night.

7. *Help each other to be right.* One of the most difficult things for teachers and school librarians can be to admit they don't know or that they might have been wrong. At the same time, it is important for students to learn that adults are people, too, and that no one is right all of the time. Be willing to listen to students, and don't be afraid to think about your response before you speak. For example, if a student asks why it is important to give a complete citation to every source used, take the time to explain how using citations helps those who read the paper judge the quality of it based on sources used in writing the paper. If a school librarian is asked a question by a student that cannot immediately be answered (e.g., why are barns painted red?), it is appropriate to admit ignorance, but follow up with helping the student find out.

8. *Be what you want students to be.* As a responsible adult in the school, the school librarian becomes a role model for the students. Therefore, it is important to model appropriate behaviors and not do anything that the students should not do. Be careful to use appropriate language, to respect students' personal space, to never talk about students where other students can overhear, and to do as much as possible to be fair to all students at all times.

9. *Play more, laugh more, and do more with them.* School is an important part of students' lives, but it does not all have to be grim. Do not be afraid to have

fun with the students. It is a good idea to attend their sports games and be involved in other recreational activities. The students will notice, and it can be very important to them. At the same time, please remember that it is a bad idea to use sarcasm with students. Younger students won't understand it, and teens often have a fragile self-image and need support, not sarcasm.

10. *Create memories that will serve students for a lifetime.* Everyone remembers some events from elementary, middle, or high school. Many of these are based on positive events. A school librarian has the opportunity to share with students and help them build memories. By being proactive and helping students to succeed, school librarians help students create positive memories. Displays of student work in the school library, one-on-one discussions of a favorite book, or helping students find information that is important to them are some of the many opportunities school librarians have to influence students.

PLANNING FOR RESILIENCE

Often, there is not one program or lesson the school librarian focuses on to help foster an authentic and caring relationship with the students. Instead, a conscious effort may be made to interact with students in a more positive and supportive way. Changes can be incorporated into lessons and individual interactions. However, the ClassMap Survey for School Libraries has a section with questions about the school librarian that is the center of the following example.

HOW CAN I FIND OUT?

I. **Scenario** (Here I describe the situation that is the issue; that I am worried about, etc.)

There was no one specific incident that sparked this project, but I felt I needed to work to strengthen my relationship with the students. First, I administered the section of the ClassMap Survey for School Librarians on "My School Librarian." (See Table 6.0.) Then, I thought about things I could do to reach out to the students, and I began to speak to each student who entered the library, tried to call each student by name, put up displays of student work, and began to ask students for the titles of books or magazines they might want in the library. Now, I want to know if my efforts had any effect.

II. **Resilience Area and Activities** (Here I decide which area of resilience to focus on and how to do that.)

I chose to focus on caring and authentic relationships between teachers and students.

III. **Question** (What is the main question I need to answer to decide whether or not the technique I chose is enhancing resilience?)

After working for this semester to reach out to students, have the scores on the ClassMap Survey for School Librarians changed?

Table 6.0
My School Librarian

1. My school librarian listens carefully to me when I talk.

| NEVER | SOMETIMES | OFTEN | ALMOST ALWAYS |

2. My school librarian helps me when I need help.

| NEVER | SOMETIMES | OFTEN | ALMOST ALWAYS |

3. My school librarian respects me.

| NEVER | SOMETIMES | OFTEN | ALMOST ALWAYS |

4. My school librarian likes having me in the school library.

| NEVER | SOMETIMES | OFTEN | ALMOST ALWAYS |

5. My school librarian makes it fun to be in the school library.

| NEVER | SOMETIMES | OFTEN | ALMOST ALWAYS |

6. My school librarian thinks I do a good job on work in the school library.

| NEVER | SOMETIMES | OFTEN | ALMOST ALWAYS |

7. My school librarian is fair to me.

| NEVER | SOMETIMES | OFTEN | ALMOST ALWAYS |

IV.   **Methodology** (How will I gather information to answer the question?)

A.   **What information do I need to gather?**
I need scores from the ClassMap Survey for School Librarians for before and after I worked to reach out to students.

B.   **How might I gather that information?**

1.   Use **existing records** or information.
Not appropriate for this question, since the ClassMap Survey was not administered prior to this semester.

2.   **Observe** what is happening.
It is possible that I will observe some changes and/or be able to cite examples of things that have happened that show the students feel comfortable with me. One student talked about a fishing trip over the weekend; another student excitedly shared information about her new puppy. But I did not record these incidents in any formal way, and so am reluctant to rely on this type of information, although some examples might be used to humanize my report.

3.   **Gather information** from people directly.

a.   **Interview**
It would be difficult to try to ask students face-to-face how they feel about their interactions with me. So, this is not an appropriate method to gather information in this case.

b. **Questionnaire**
I will use the ClassMaps Survey for School Librarians included in this book. Students will complete the section on "School Librarian" at the beginning of the semester and at the end of the semester. This focuses directly on student perceptions of the school librarians, and it allows students to give anonymous responses.

c. **Test**
Not appropriate for this situation because I am interested in perceptions instead of learning.

d. **Assignment or Exercise**
Not appropriate for this situation because I want to better understand how students feel about me instead of the effectiveness of my teaching.

C. Collect the data (using the technique I identified previously).
Students were asked to fill out the following section from the ClassMaps Survey for School Librarians at the beginning of the semester. Then, they were asked to fill out the same questions again 14 weeks later.

V. **Data Analysis** (Now what do I do with all this information?)
The data are in Table 6.1. Further analysis needs to be done to find patterns.

A. **Numbers**

1. **Frequencies**
Frequencies are the number of times a certain category was chosen. If the four categories of choices are compared for the first and second times the students filled out the questionnaire, it would look like Table 6.2.

Table 6.1
Summary of Student Responses to ClassMap Survey

Question	Never		Sometimes		Often		Almost Always	
	1st	2nd	1st	2nd	1st	2nd	1st	2nd
Listens carefully to me when I talk	2	0	8	3	8	9	2	8
Helps me when I need help	0	0	2	0	8	8	10	12
Respects me	2	0	8	3	8	9	2	8
Likes having me in the school library	2	0	10	5	8	5	0	10
Makes it fun to be in the school library	4	0	6	2	5	10	5	8
Thinks I do a good job on work	4	0	4	2	10	10	2	8
Is fair to me	0	0	2	0	14	10	4	10

Examination of the table indicates that student perceptions of the school librarian are more favorable at the end of the semester than they were at the beginning of the semester.

2. **Bar graphs**

A bar graph based on Table 6.2 would look like Figure 6.1.

Sometimes, it can be useful to look at each question. In that case, it is possible to create a graph for each individual question. Figure 6.2 is for the second question, "My school librarian helps me when I need help."

Table 6.2
Student Ratings of School Librarian Behavior

Rating	First Test	Second Test
Never	14	0
Sometimes	40	15
Often	61	61
Almost Always	25	64

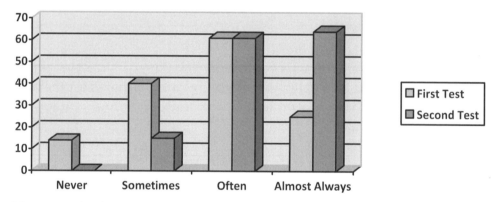

Figure 6.1: Student ratings of school librarian behavior.

My school librarian helps me when I need help.

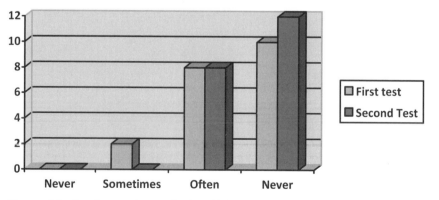

Figure 6.2: Student ratings of school librarian helpfulness.

Table 6.3
Percentage of Responses in Each Category

Category	First Test	Second Test
Never	10%	0%
Sometimes	29%	11%
Often	44%	44%
Almost Always	18%	46%

I can create an individual graph for each of the questions in the ClassMap Survey if I wish to more closely examine the data.

3. **Percentages**

I can calculate the percentage of responses in each category. See Table 6.3.

Sometimes I find that percentages are more effective to compare two separate categories because the numbers are not as large.

4. **Pie graph**

While this will show the percentage for each time the questionnaire was administered, it is not a good technique to use to compare the two different sets of questionnaires, because that would total to 200 percent instead of the 100 percent of one questionnaire.

5. **Change over time**

Sometimes the line graph is a good way to find change over time. However, it is best used for data such as prices where the data is continuous. (For example, if I look for a price between $1.00 and $2.00, the answer of $1.50 makes sense. There is no such midpoint between "Never" and "Sometimes.")

B. **Observations**

Not really a major source of data for this project because I did not use an observation instrument.

C. **Interviews and Questionnaires**

1. **Closed questions**

In this case, the data were available in numbers from the questionnaire used. See section V. A, "Numbers."

2. **Open questions**

No open questions were used.

VI. **What does this tell me about my original question?**

From the results of the questionnaire, it appears that my efforts have been effective. There has definitely been improvement in the scores on the second test as compared to the first test. I have also noticed that more students take the time to talk with me about things going on in their lives or books they have read.

VII. **Using the information.**

   A. How does this help me make decisions or better understand resilience in my school library?

   Based on the results, I think my efforts to reach out to the students have been effective. The majority of the responses on the second questionnaire are in the "often" and " almost always" categories. Analysis of individual questions shows that students already felt fairly comfortable asking for help, although that has improved, too. My efforts have been most successful in the area of making the school library a welcoming place to be.

   B. Use the information to decide whether to continue the current activity, make changes to the current activity, or devise and implement another activity.

   The changes I made definitely had an impact on the students. I will try to continue to reach out to the students and enhance the positive atmosphere I have begun to create.

   C. Share the information with students, teachers, and administrators.

   It can be beneficial to share the results of the questionnaire with students so they understand what I am trying to do and how they have responded. This is another way to show them that I am interested in them. It might be valuable (depending on the personalities of the people involved) to share this information with other teachers or administrators.

REFERENCES

Assor, A., Kaplan, H., & Roth, G. (2002). Choice is good, but relevance is excellent: Autonomy-enhancing and suppressing teacher behaviours predicting students' engagement in schoolwork. *British Journal of Educational Psychology, 72,* 261–278.

Bear, G. C., Cavalier, A. R., & Manning, M. (2005). *Developing self-discipline and preventing and correcting misbehavior.* Boston: Pearson/Allyn & Bacon.

Birch, S. H., & Ladd, G. W. (1997). The teacher-child relationship and children's early school adjustment. *Journal of School Psychology, 35,* 61–79.

Birch, S. H., & Ladd, G. W. (1998). Children's interpersonal behaviors and the teacher-child relationship. *Developmental Psychology, 34,* 934–946.

Brekelmans, M., Wubbels, T., & Levy, J. (1993). Student performance, attitudes, instructional strategies and teacher-communication style. In T. Wubbels & J. Levy (Eds.), *Do you know what you look like? Interpersonal relationships in education* (pp. 56–63). Washington, DC: The Falmer Press.

Brooks, R. B., & Goldstein, S. (2007). Developing the mindset of effective teachers. In S. Goldstein, & R. B. Brooks (Eds.), *Understanding and managing children's classroom behavior: Creating sustainable, resilient classrooms* (2nd ed., pp. 189–207). Hoboken, NJ: John Wiley & Sons.

Christenson, S. L., & Anderson, A. R. (2002). Commentary: The centrality of the learning for students' academic enabler skills. *School Psychology Review, 31*(3), 378–394.

Doll, B., LeClair, C., & Kurien, S. (2009). Effective classrooms: Classroom learning environments that foster school success. In T. Gutkin & C. Reynolds (Eds.), *The handbook of school psychology* (pp. 791–807). Hoboken, NJ: John Wiley & Sons.

Epstein, J., & Sheldon, S. B. (2002). Present and accounted for: Improving student attendance through family and community involvement. *Journal of Educational Research, 95*(5), 308–318.

Hamre, B. K., & Pianta, R. C. (2005). Can instructional and emotional support in the first-grade classroom make a difference for children at risk of school failure? *Child Development, 76*(5), 949–967.

Karns, M. (1994). *How to create positive relationships with students: A handbook of group activities and teaching strategies.* Champaign, IL: Research Press.

Kesner, J. E. (2000). Teacher characteristics and the quality of child-teacher relationships. *Journal of School Psychology, 28,* 133–149.

Pianta, R. C. (1999). *Enhancing relationships between children and teachers.* Washington, DC: American Psychological Association.

Pianta, R. C., & Stuhlman, M. W. (2004). Teacher-child relationships and children's success in the first years of school. *School Psychology Review, 33,* 444–458.

Resnick, M. D., Bearman, P. S., Blum, R. W., Bauman, K. E., Harris, K. M., Jones, J., et al. (1997). Protecting adolescents from harm: Findings from the National Longitudinal Study on Adolescent Health. *Journal of the American Medical Association, 278,* 823–832.

Roeser, R. W., Midgley, C., & Urdan, T. C. (1996). Perceptions of the school psychological environment and early adolescents' psychological and behavioral functioning in school: The mediating role of goals and belonging. *Journal of Educational Psychology, 88*(3), 408–422.

Walker, T. W. (2008). Looking at teacher practices through the lens of parenting style. *The Journal of Experimental Education, 76*(2), 218–240.

Wentzel, K. R. (2002). Are effective teachers like good parents? Teaching styles and student adjustment in early adolescence. *Child Development, 73*(1), 287–301.

Werner, E. E. (2006). What can we learn about resilience from large-scale longitudinal studies? In S. Goldstein & R. B. Brooks (Eds.), *Handbook of resilience in children* (pp. 91–105). New York: Springer Publishing.

7

The Role of Peer Relationships in Resilience

Children's relationships with their peers are essential links that bond them to schools, contribute mightily to their enjoyment of learning, support them through difficult times, and strengthen their social competence (Doll & Brehm, 2010). Wentzel (2005) notes, "Relationships with peers are of central importance to children throughout childhood and adolescence. They provide a source of companionship and entertainment, help in solving problems, personal validation and emotional support, and especially during adolescence, a foundation for identity development" (Brown, Mory, & Kinney, 1994; and Parker & Asher, 1993, cited in Wentzel, 2005, p. 279). Four aspects of peer relationships are critical to students' success: (1) their capacity to form and maintain rewarding friendships with peers (peer friendships), (2) their reputation as socially acceptable by their classmates (peer acceptance), (3) their capacity to resolve the inevitable conflicts that they will have with classmates and particularly with friends, and (4) their ability to protect themselves from intimidation and bullying by older or more powerful students (Doll & Brehm, 2010; Pellegrini, 2005).

Friendships are identified when two students choose each other as a friend, choose to spend time together, and the relationship persists over time (Asher, Parker, & Walker, 1996). Early friendships formed in preschool or the early elementary grades tend to be "convenience" friendships in which children play and converse with other children who are most available to them: classmates, sons and daughters of their parents' friends, or neighborhood children (Doll, 1996; Pellegrini & Blatchford, 2000). By second or third grade, students show a decided preference for friends who share their interests and exchange favors or special privileges with them—saving them a seat at lunch, walking together to and from school, or playing together at recess. With age and maturity, the favors that friends exchange become more abstract—providing a listening ear, standing up for each other, staying loyal, and acting in each other's best interest. Making friends requires that students spend some time having fun together. Often, this occurs naturally when either child approaches the other and suggests that they play. However, some students are easily intimidated and struggle to take this first step, even though all students tend to seek friendships among readily available classmates. Adults can encourage friendships by creating opportunities for students to work or play together.

Keeping friends requires that students be good friends by helping each other, sharing possessions, and caring for each other—but these prosocial skills are not sufficient (Doll, 1996). Conflict and aggression also play a special role in students' friendships. Conflicts among peers are inevitable in that individual students frequently have competing interests or needs, and students' capacity to fully understand the perspectives of other children is somewhat limited by their as-yet-immature sociocognitive abilities (Blatchford, Baines, & Pellegrini, 2003; Pellegrini & Smith, 1998). Indeed, most students' conflicts occur between students and their friends and not between students and nonfriends—understandable given that most of students' time is spent with their friends (Doll, 1996). The mark of good friendships is not to prevent all of the conflicts from occurring in the first place because many of these erupt unexpectedly and suddenly. Instead, good friends are effective at *repairing* the conflicts—at taking back an unintended insult, suggesting a compromise, giving in, and apologizing. Adults can promote the continuation of friendships by providing "scripts" that students can use to talk through conflicts and arrive at a mutual solution.

Peer aggression and conflicts are challenging for students in another respect. Watch any two good friends together for a period of time, and it will be obvious that they call each other names, practice insults, tease each other, rough house and play fight, and generally act out the kind of aggressive behaviors that make adults cringe (Blatchford et al., 2003; Pellegrini & Smith, 1998). If a teacher or other adult objects and interrupts the students' play, they are quick to complain, "but we were just messing around." Friendship researchers call this "jostling" or "rough and tumble play," and its occurrence has been documented across ages, gender, and ethnicity. Indeed, jostling makes it particularly difficult for adult observers to interpret students' play because the same apparent behaviors lead to fighting and hurt feelings when they occur between nonfriends, and are tolerated and even encouraged from friends. Thus, students must not only be able to judge which social behaviors are appropriate, but to understand how the social rules shift depending on whether the other child is a friend, acquaintance, stranger, or enemy (Doll, 1996). Occasionally, even the students become confused and some misunderstandings among friends have begun when an action that one child intended to be "messing around" was interpreted by the other child as "doing it to be mean." These social misunderstandings are the frequent topic of children's literature, and their resolution often depends on students talking through what occurred—much like would occur in an engaging book club discussion.

Peer acceptance is not the same as friendship. "Peer acceptance is operationally assessed by determining the degree to which members of a group like a child and want to spend time with him or her" (Doll, 1996, p. 166). If all students in a class rate their classmates according to how much they want to spend time together, four groups of students can be identified (Asher et al., 1996). Popular students are those who are identified as a preferred partner by many of their classmates. In many cases, popular students are those who are particularly positive and caring, but this is not always the case. Some popular students appear to be quite aggressive, and their popularity seems to be due to the inordinate social power that they wield. Rejected students are those who are actively disliked by many of their classmates. Many of these rejected students are particularly aggressive or difficult, and their disturbing behaviors disrupt the play of their classmates. However, other students appear to be rejected because they have unusual or unattractive mannerisms or appearance. Neglected students are those who are neither liked nor disliked by their classmates; instead, they appear to be invisible students whose presence in the classroom is rarely noticed. Many neglected students are very withdrawn and socially anxious, and they may need assistance forming and keeping friends. They may share few interests in common with their classmates and find it difficult to enjoy the activities that other students enjoy. Adults frequently believe that neglected students are intentionally withdrawn because they would rather be alone, but a more accurate assessment is that they lack confidence in their own ability to carry a friendship and are reluctant to take social risks (Doll, 1996; Doll & Brehm, 2010). Typical students are liked by some classmates, disliked by a few, have at least three mutual friends, and are generally satisfied with their social lives at school. Most students spend much of their free time (recess, lunch, or before and after school) playing contentedly with classmates.

A particular challenge for adults and students is bullying, or instances in which more powerful children repeatedly intimidate, threaten, or hurt less powerful children who are unable to defend themselves (Batsche & Porter, 2006). In addition to the bullying child, onlookers may contribute to bullying by encouraging or participating, and adults may inadvertently facilitate bullying when they fail to interrupt or stop intimidation when they see it. Bullying is common enough that most students have observed other students being bullied or have experienced it themselves. Indeed, in any typical group of students, ask how many students have picked on someone else "just to be mean," and lots of hands will go up. Ultimately, bullying is damaging to all of its participants—the students who are victimized, the onlookers who witness bullying or participate, and the bullying students whose long-term friendships and mental health are damaged. School practices that discourage bullying include posting prominent rules against peer bullying, vigilant efforts by teachers and other adults to stop bullying when it occurs, strong friendship networks among all students in the school so that students are protected from bullying by their friends, diligent efforts by onlooking students who have been taught how to stop students from bullying other classmates, and instruction in empowering strategies for students who are bullied so that they know how to get help (Doll & Swearer, 2006).

Wentzel (2005) identifies "peer defined social competence [as] one of frequent displays of prosocial behavior (e.g., helping, sharing, caring), relatively infrequent displays of antisocial and disruptive behavior, and some modicum of academic success" (p. 284). Socially competent students will have at least three good friends to play with and spend time with, will contribute in positive and prosocial ways to those friendships, will be able to resolve the occasional peer conflict that they encounter, will have earned the social acceptance of the majority of their classmates, and will neither participate in nor be easily victimized by bullying behaviors of other students (Doll & Brehm, 2010). Simply setting and enforcing rules for positive social behaviors is not enough to support this broadly defined social competence. In addition, students also benefit when adults create opportunities for them to have fun with their classmates; provide systematic, step-by-step strategies for resolving peer conflicts when these occur; lead reflective group discussions of the frequent social accidents and misunderstandings that occur between friends; encourage more capable or socially powerful students to set goals to act in ways that protect and care for students who are isolated or victimized; and set and diligently enforce prohibitions against bullying.

While academic accomplishments are positively correlated with peer approval and acceptance, research as yet has not shown that peer acceptance results in higher grades (Wentzel, 2005). However, longitudinal studies have shown that students who had no friends in fourth grade were significantly more likely as young adults to leave school without graduating, be dishonorably discharged from the military, or struggle with emotional disturbances (Doll, 1996). More immediately, having friends at school highly influences participation in school activities and a feeling of belonging, and this, in turn, prompts students to actively engage in learning (National Research Council & the Institute of Medicine, 2004). Conversely, students who experience peer rejection have more feelings of loneliness and dissatisfaction, and their participation in classroom learning falters (Christenson & Anderson, 2002).

SUGGESTIONS

In the school library, there are numerous modifications of routines and practices that support positive peer relationships among students. Informal routines offer the students nonmandatory encouragement to affiliate with their peers. Formal interventions can be integrated into instructional design or into the school library program.

Facilities

Researchers in the field of environmental psychology study the way people react in a particular physical setting. In his work, Thompson (1973) noted that students seated at tables tend to interact more with each other more than students seated at individual locations, such as carrels, or at square tables. Therefore, students may either avoid round tables (if they came to work) or seek out round tables (if they came for interaction or group work). It is true that individual space is important to some students at some times and for some types of assignments or assessments. For example, one high school student frequently came to the school library from study hall. Some days, he would sit at a table and interact with other students. Other days, he would seek a place to sit alone and read. At the same time, in order to foster and support peer interactions in the school library, there should be some tables where the students can gather to visit and/or work together. Observation is one appropriate technique to use to record the number of students using the tables and the type of interactions occurring there. When rearranging furniture or purchasing new furniture to facilitate group work, keep track of student interaction in the school library before and after the changes.

School libraries that welcome students and where students feel comfortable also support student interaction. The facility should be bright and pleasing in both appearance and atmosphere. Rules and regulations are necessary, but they should not be overly restrictive. Casual browsing materials in the collection, such as gaming or fashion magazines, demonstrate that students are welcome. When updating and refining the facilities and collections, record the number of students in the school library and note the type and frequency of their interactions with other students both before and after the changes.

Extracurricular Activities

There are numerous extracurricular activities that could be hosted in the school library, such as game day. By providing additional opportunities for students to have fun together, these activities can strengthen student friendships and promote a stronger social climate in the school. One option is for these activities to be scheduled after school, if there is support for this within the educational community. "[I]nterviews with resilient students suggest that participating in after-school programs may well contribute to students' social competence and interpersonal skills" (Cove, Eiseman, & Popkin, 2005, p. 13). These types of activities are a more formalized extension of the welcoming atmosphere necessary for resilient libraries. Talking with the students is one way to identify the types of activities they would welcome, or a more formal survey could be done. It is important to follow through and actually schedule some of these activities that the students identify. More students will be involved if a variety of different activities are scheduled that appeal to different audiences. Again, observe student attendance and involvement in the activities to gather information about the impact of the activities.

Book Clubs

Book clubs provide students the opportunity to read and talk about the books they are reading, and they also give students the opportunity to interact with their peers. In many cases, youth literature directly addresses difficulties in peer relationships that students are facing in their daily lives, and it provides them with opportunities to examine and identify solutions for disturbing peer problems related to making and keeping friends, resolving minor conflicts with peers, or confronting bullying and intimidation. Voluntary book clubs could meet before school, during the lunch hour or activity period, or after school. Whether to host a book club in a school library or not depends on the situation. If student interest is high and the principal supports activities that encourage leisure reading, book clubs may be appropriate. Remember that because this is a voluntary activity, some of the students who would benefit most from the opportunity to interact with their peers may not wish to join. To gauge the effectiveness of the book club, it is possible to keep attendance, record observations of student interactions, or survey the students.

Peer Support

There are some practical things that can be done in the school library that can foster students' peer relationships (Doll, 1996). One of these is to encourage students to ask each other before approaching the school librarian for clarification or information when working. For example, post signs in the school library that list appropriate ways for students to ask for help. Be sure to include "other students" on the list of appropriate people to ask for help; this list may also include the school librarian, a teacher, or another adult working in the school library. Also, students can be orally reminded that it is okay to ask other students for help. Asking students to seek and give help to each other can easily be incorporated into lessons taught in the school library. One way to gauge the effectiveness of this approach is to observe students in the school library. Another way would be to include a section on the student assignment or worksheet asking how many of their fellow students asked them for help and also how many students they asked for help. In one situation, the school librarian worked with individual students to follow the steps to identify and then locate materials needed for a school assignment. By the end of the school year, numerous students were showing their classmates how to do this.

Cooperative Learning

Creating pairings or groupings of students that require them to complete tasks cooperatively can give additional opportunities for peer interactions (Doll, 1996). This can be done informally, by telling students to work together to complete their worksheets, or students may be grouped in advance of the lesson.

One technique that supports peer interactions is cooperative learning. Indeed, research indicates, "cooperative learning was highly related to social support within the classroom and that the longer and more frequently students engaged in cooperative learning, the greater the social support within the classroom" (Johnson, Johnson, Buckman, & Richards, 2001, p. 405). One student in a library and information science class, who worked in a school that stresses cooperative learning, reported that special education students are more accepted by and integrated into peer relationships in classrooms where cooperative learning techniques are applied. Cooperative learning provides students the opportunity to interact with their peers, creates opportunities for peer acceptance, and promotes positive relationships between students (Rottier & Ogan, 1991). Teachers and school librarians must be proactive in creating groups for cooperative learning and teaching students how to participate in cooperative learning activities. Chapter 9 explores cooperative learning techniques in more depth.

Observations can be used to gather information about the effect of cooperative learning on peer relationships. Another technique is to ask the students, perhaps using an anonymous survey. While not a direct measure of peer relationships, it could be useful to note the effect of cooperative learning on individual performance as shown on assignments or other group products.

Peer Tutoring

Peer tutoring is a formalized pairing of students to work on specific structured learning events, such as quizzing each other on spelling words. It provides opportunities for peer interactions, but it also has other benefits. For example, in a study of fourth and fifth grade students, a reciprocal peer tutoring method was designed where paired students took turns tutoring each other. They discovered that students who were peer teachers developed significantly higher levels of academic efficacy and behavioral self-control than students who were not peer teachers. Classwide Peer Tutoring (CWPT) is another system allowing students to learn together. In CWPT, pairs of students work together practicing and quizzing each other on academic tasks and providing each other with immediate feedback. Research and personal experience indicate that CWPT increases student time on task, improves academic performance, and increases cooperation and other social skills (Greenwood, Delquadri, & Carta, 1997). In another peer tutoring study, high achieving girls were paired with boys with attention deficit hyperactivity disorder (ADHD) in an elementary school (Wentzel & Watkins, 2002). Each pair planned routes to purchase all items on two separate lists, and as a result, the boys showed academic gains. These forms of peer-assisted learning benefited students' academic achievement and their peer relationships, and the tutors benefited as well as the students who were tutored (Fantuzzo & Rohrbeck, 1992). Again, more details and suggestions are included in Chapter 9.

Literature Circles

Literature circles are structured learning events where a group of students read the same book and then meet to discuss one or more aspects of the book using questions or activities prepared in advance. The technique has been used successfully with students from the primary grades through college. This is another instructional technique that can be used to promote peer interactions. As with other techniques, it is important to "teach" students how to participate in literature circles. Observation is appropriate in this case, also, to gather information on how students interact with each other in literature circles. More details are available in Chapter 9.

PLANNING FOR RESILIENCE

As in other chapters, it is important to evaluate the effectiveness of the strategies developed and implemented. One of the most effective ways to do this for peer relationships is to observe student behavior.

HOW CAN I FIND OUT?

I. **Scenario** (Here I describe the situation that is the issue; that I am worried about, etc.)

This year I have worked with the tenth grade English teacher to use literature circles with the students to discuss the required reading in class. We first used the literature circle discussion techniques and roles in whole class discussions, and then we created groups for later literature circle discussions. At first, we created discussion questions, but later we had the students create their own questions. We read about resilience and decided to use the literature circles to try to improve peer relationships among the students.

II. **Resilience Area and Activities** (Here I decide which area of resilience to focus on and how to do that.)

The area of resilience we focused on was peer relationships, and we used literature circles this year with a tenth grade English class.

III. **Question** (What is the main question I need to answer to decide whether or not the technique I chose is enhancing resilience?)

Have peer relationships strengthened this year as a result of participation in literature circles?

IV. **Methodology** (How will I gather information to answer the question?)

A. **What information do I need to gather?**
We need to find a way to evaluate the peer relationships among the students and the types of interactions that occur.

B. **How might I gather that information?**

1. Use **existing records** or information.
Not appropriate in this case.

2. **Observe** what is happening.
A form will be designed to use as we observe the students interacting with each other as they work in literature circles.

3. **Gather information** from people directly.

a. **Interview**
Not appropriate because students would probably not feel comfortable discussing their opinions of and reactions to their classmates directly with either the teacher or the school librarian.

b. **Questionnaire**
We decided not to use a survey in this case. We were interested in what actually happened (observation) and not in what students felt or believed (questionnaire).

c. **Test**
Not appropriate in this case.

d. **Assignment or Exercise**
Not appropriate in this case because we are not interested in how much the students learn. Instead we are interested in the relationships among students.

C. Collect the data (using the technique I identified previously).
We decided that observations were the best method to assess the effect of literature circles on peer interactions. We assigned the students to groups of three or four for the discussions. To record our observations of students and groups, we used the following form. As the groups were discussing the assigned book, the teacher and school librarian observed the groups and filled out a form for each group. We used the form for the five literature circle experiences across the course of the year. The teacher and school librarian could just fill in the number representing the level/quality of interaction while circulating around the room. It was decided that individual student names were not necessary because we were interested in overall student interactions and not focusing on only one individual.

Circle Observation Form: Tenth Grade English Class

Group _____Date _____

Observation Category				
Group as a Whole				
worked well together				
supported each other in discussion and arguments				
stayed focused on the book				
tried to include everyone in the discussion				
Individual Students	**Student 1**	**Student 2**	**Student 3**	**Student 4**
was prepared for the discussion				
respected contributions of others				
asked questions to encourage discussion				
contributed thoughtful ideas to the discussion				
competently carried out assigned role for this discussion				
built on the comments of others in the group				

Scale: 1 = Performed well overall in interactions with other group members

2 = Some interactions were at optimal/acceptable level; some room for improvement

3 = Deficient in some way

V. **Data Analysis** (Now what do I do with all this information?)

A. **Numbers**

1. **Frequencies**

   Because we were looking for change, we decided to compare the total number of rating in each category from the first and from the fifth (and last) literature circle. There were 18 students in the class, and we formed three groups of 4 and two groups of 3. Each group received two ratings—one from the teacher and one from the school librarian. Here is a table of those results:

Frequency of Ratings for Group Observations

Observation Area	1st Observation			5th Observation		
	1	2	3	1	2	3
Worked well together	8	16	12	12	16	8
Supported each other	5	16	15	5	17	14
Stayed focused on the book	16	17	3	28	6	2
Included everyone in discussions	9	19	8	12	16	8

2. **Bar graphs**

   Bar graphs for each of the four categories used to judge the group cohesiveness are given in Figures 7.1 through 7.4. They visually represent the data given in the previous table. Four separate graphs are needed to adequately represent all four areas used on the observation form. Remember that 1 is the high score, and a score of 3 indicates some deficiencies.

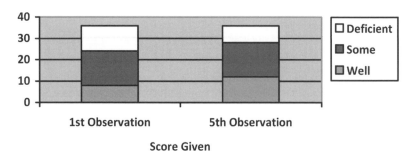

Figure 7.1: Ratings for "Worked Well Together."

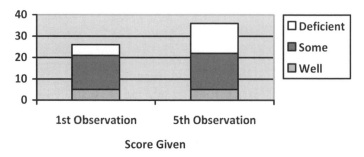

Figure 7.2: Ratings for "Support Each Other."

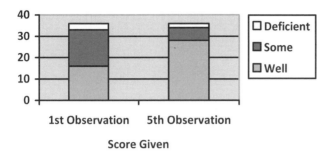

Figure 7.3: Ratings for "Stay Focused on the Book."

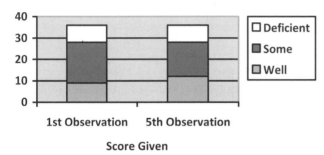

Figure 7.4: Ratings for "Include Everyone."

3. **Percentages**

Not necessary in this case, although I could calculate them if I felt they would be useful.

4. **Pie graph**

Again, not necessary in this case, although I could calculate them if I felt they would be useful.

5. **Change over time**

The bar graphs capture the changes visually. There is no need for a line graph on these data.

B. **Observations**

In this case, the observations were recorded as numbers, and so have been compiled and examined in Section A above.

C. Interviews & Questionnaires

Not used in this case.

VI. **What does this tell me about my original question?**

Examination of the numbers in the tables and of the bar graphs shows there was little change in the group activities as observed by the teacher and the school librarian, with one exception. By the fifth observation, the groups were doing a much better job of keeping the discussions focused on the book instead of merely chit-chatting. Other areas analyzed (working well together, supporting each other, and including everyone in the discussions) show only minor changes. It is hard to tell why there is not more change in the areas examined. Together, the teacher and I have brainstormed possible reasons for the observed lack of change:

- Students participated in only five literature circles. This may not have provided enough time for structured interaction to have a greater effect on the observed interactions.

- The observation instrument may not be structured to identify the changes that did occur.

- Effects may have been too minor to be detected by the observation instrument.

- Effects may have occurred outside of the literature circle environment and so were not observed and recorded.

- The type of change we were trying to effect may be too far removed from the literature circle environment to be detected by this procedure.

VII. Using the information.

   A. How does this help me make decisions or better understand resilience in my school library?

   Unfortunately, we were unable to document changes in peer relationships among the students participating in the literature circles. Anecdotal evidence (comments made by students, interactions between group members outside of the literature circle time) indicates there were some positive effects. At this time, no firm conclusions can be reached about the effectiveness of literature circles on peer relationships.

   B. Use the information to decide whether to continue the current activity, make changes to the current activity, or devise and implement another activity.

   The teacher and I both believe the literature circles are an effective instructional technique to prompt students to discuss required reading in the class. So, we will continue to use the literature circles and will also work to redesign the observation instrument. Next time, we will also adapt and use the classmates section of the ClassMaps discussed in Chapter 2 of this book.

   C. Share the information with students, teachers, and administrators.

   The teacher and I believe that literature circles were effective, and we plan to continue using them. I will suggest literature circles as an appropriate instructional technique in collaborative planning with other teachers.

REFERENCES

Asher, S. R., Parker, J. G., & Walker, D. L. (1996). Distinguishing friendship from acceptance: Implications for intervention and assessment. In W. M. Bukowski, A. F. Newcomb, &

W. W. Hartup (Eds.), *The company they keep: Friendship in childhood and adolescence* (pp. 366–405). New York: Cambridge Press.

Batsche, G., & Porter, L. (2006). Bullying. In G. Bear & K. Minke (Eds.), *Children's needs III: Development, problems, and alternatives* (pp. 135–148). Bethesda, MD: National Association of School Psychologists.

Blatchford, P., Baines, E., & Pellegrini, A. (2003). The social context of school playground games: Sex and ethnic differences and changes over time after entry to junior school. *British Journal of Developmental Psychology, 21,* 481–505.

Brown, B. B., Mory, M. S., & Kinney, D. (1994) Casting adolescent crowds in a relational perspective: Caricature, channel and context. In R. Montemayor, G. R. Adams, & T. P. Gullotta (Eds.), *Personal relationships during adolescence* (pp. 123–167). Newbury Park, CA: Sage.

Christenson, S. L., & Anderson, A. R. (2002). Commentary: The centrality of the learning for students' academic enabler skills. *School Psychology Review, 31*(3), 378–394.

Cove, E., Eiseman, M., & Popkin, S. J. (2005, December). *Resilient Children: Literature Review and Evidence from the HOPE VI Panel Study; Final Report.* New York: The Ford Foundation Community and Resource Development.

Doll, B. (1996). Children without friends: Implications for practice and policy. *School Psychology Review, 25*(2), 165–182.

Doll, B., & Brehm, K. (2010). *Resilient playgrounds.* New York: Routledge.

Doll, B., & Swearer, S. (2006). Cognitive-behavioral interventions for participants in bullying and coercion. In R. Mennuti, A. Freeman, & R. Christner (Eds.), *Cognitive behavioral interventions in educational settings: A handbook for practice* (pp. 183–201). New York: Brunner-Routledge.

Fantuzzo, J. W., & Rohrbeck, C. A. (1992). Self-managed groups: Fitting self-management approaches into classroom systems. *School Psychology Review, 21*(2), 255–264.

Greenwood, C. R., Delquadri, J. C., & Carta, J. J. (1997). *Together we can! Classwide peer tutoring to improve basic academic skills.* Longmont, CO: Sopris West.

Johnson, D. W., Johnson, R. T., Buckman, L. A., & Richards, P. S. (2001). The effect of prolonged implementation of cooperative learning on social support within the classroom. *The Journal of Psychology, 119*(5), 405–411.

National Research Council and the Institute of Medicine. (2004). *Engaging schools: Fostering high school students' motivation to learn.* Committee on Increasing High School Students' Engagement and Motivation to Learn; Board on Children, Youth, and Families; Division of Behavioral and Social Sciences and Education. Washington, DC: The National Academies Press.

Parker, J. G. & Asher, S. R. (1993). Friendship and friendship quality in middle childhood: Links with peer group acceptance and feelings of loneliness and social dissatisfaction. *Developmental Psychology, 29,* 611–621.

Pellegrini, A. D. (2005). *Recess: Its role in education and development.* Mahwah, NJ: Lawrence Erlbaum.

Pellegrini, A.D., & Blatchford, P. (2000). *The child at school: Interactions with peers and teachers.* New York: Oxford University Press.

Pellegrini, A.D., & Smith, P.K. (1998). Physical activity play: The nature and function of a neglected aspect of play. *Child Development, 69,* 577–598.

Rottier, J., & Ogan, B.J. (1991). *Cooperative learning in middle-level schools.* Washington, DC: National Education Association.

Thompson, J.J. (1973). *Beyond words: Nonverbal communication in the classroom.* New York: Citation Press.

Wentzel, K.R. (2005). Peer relationships, motivation, and academic performance at school. In A.J. Elliot & C.S. Dweck (Eds.), *Handbook of competence and motivation* (pp. 279–296). New York: Guilford Press.

Wentzel, K.R., & Watkins, D.E. (2002). Peer relationships and collaborative learning as contexts for academic enablers. *School Psychology Review, 31*(3), 366–377.

8

The Role of Family in Resilience

The sixth characteristic of learning environments that promotes resilience in children is a strong and comfortable partnership between schools and families, evident when families know about and reinforce school routines and practices and when schools are familiar with and sensitive to families' values and goals for their children. As noted by Christenson and Anderson (2002), "resilience is not a property of children, but resides in the interactions, transactions, and relationships among the multiple systems that envelop children. Therefore, child competence is understood in terms of co-action, the dynamic influence of relationships among child, home, school, peer and neighborhood systems" (p. 382).

Engaging schools engage families as well as students (Carter & Wojtkiewicz, 2000), a phenomenon that Comer, Haynes, Joyner, and Ben-Avie (1996) call "rallying the whole village." When schools are managed so that families and the immediate community are welcome partners in school services and decisions, families reinforce the values that strengthen students' active participation in schooling. Engaged students are not only present in the classroom, but show effort and persistence in their work and embrace the goals of learning, value school success, and believe that success in school will prepare them for success in jobs, family responsibilities, and community lives.

At a minimum, engaged students must be present in schools; family involvement research has examined strategies to improve students' daily attendance and reduce chronic absenteeism. Some of the successful strategies were school-based, such as giving awards to students for attendance (e.g., parties, certificates, recognition at assemblies) or involving students in after-school activities. However, many other successful strategies strengthened the communication between home and school by making more effective or more frequent efforts to interact with families, designating a single person from the school to contact family members with questions or concerns, providing workshops for parents, and visiting the family in their home to discuss their child's well-being (Carter & Wojtkiewicz, 2000).

Authentically engaged students are not only present in the classroom but actively participate in learning by paying attention, completing assignments, accruing credits toward graduation, and mastering the school curricula. One of the most effective programs to repair the school success of disengaged students, the Check and Connect program (Christenson & Reschly, 2010; Sinclair, Christenson, Evelo, & Hurley, 1998), has as its cornerstone strengthening the communication between the schools and families of students at risk of dropping out of school. A Check and Connect mentor continuously tracks student absences, tardies, truancies, grades and credits, and behavioral referrals. Through ongoing collaboration, students and their families are provided with regular feedback about students' educational progress, reminded frequently of the importance of staying in school, and helped to solve some of the problems that interfere with students' school performance. After two years of enrollment in the program, 91 percent of the Check and Connect students were still in school at the end of ninth grade, compared to 70 percent of students in a control group.

"It is well established that parental school involvement has a positive influence on school-related outcomes for children. Consistently, cross-sectional and longitudinal studies have demonstrated an association between higher levels of parental school involvement and greater academic success for children and adolescents" (Hill & Taylor, 2004, p. 161). To date most studies have focused on the role of mothers, and less work has been done with fathers. Some research indicates that parents of adolescent boys provided more homework supervision than parents of girls (Shumow & Miller, 2001). Other research shows that adolescent daughters received more parental involvement on four variables: discussions about school, higher expectations for educational attainment, amount of time allowed to socialize with friends, and attendance at school events in which the student participated (Carter & Wojtkiewicz, 2000). For adolescent sons, there were significantly more frequent parent–school interactions (researchers hypothesize this might be due to behavior problems), and parents were significantly more likely to check homework.

Families, too, play an essential role in strengthening the home–school partnership. Certain family activities come immediately to mind as examples of family involvement in schools: attending parent conferences, coming to back-to-school night, or attending students' school performances. However, the research on family involvement identifies a much wider variety of activities that can be classified as family involvement and that occur both in school and in the home. "Such diverse activities as volunteering in the classroom, communicating with the teacher, participating in academic-related activities at home, communicating the positive value of education, and participating in the parent-teacher relationship are all included in parental school involvement, and each is related to school performance" (Hill & Taylor, 2004, p. 163). Other types of involvement include monitoring or assisting with homework, discussing school activities with students, participating in parent–teacher organizations, interacting with teachers via phone or e-mail, or serving on committees or boards (Shumow & Miller, 2001). All of these examples of parent involvement are most powerful when students know that they are occurring and recognize that their families are working in concert with the school to promote the students' achievement and success.

Research has identified some characteristics of parents who are less involved with their children's education. For example, there is some evidence that the amount of at-school parental involvement differs by educational level, with more parental involvement when students are in the elementary grades than secondary grades. Another common finding of the research is that "parents of successful students were involved more at school than were parents of either average students or struggling students" (Shumow & Miller, 2001, p. 85). Also noteworthy, less-educated parents are not as likely as more educated parents to advocate for their children or adolescents at school (Shumow & Miller, 2001). Parents who are less involved in their children's schools may be uncomfortable with schools and teachers, or they may believe that they cannot successfully help their child in school, or there may be some other reason for their uninvolvement. Families with limited resources might be less present in school because they are struggling against logistical barriers like limited transportation, inflexible work schedules, or multiple jobs; or they might have a personal history of school failure or conflict.

Still, interpretation of these findings must be made with caution. Almost all of this research is correlational in design, and results have not determined whether parental involvement results in more successful students, or students' poor performance in school discourages their parents from being more involved. Results of existing research are also highly dependent on how each study described and assessed "parent involvement." For example, one recent study showed that fathers were just as involved as mothers in their children's school as long as "parent involvement" included at-home activities in support of school—such as monitoring homework, discouraging television watching, or enforcing bedtimes. Thus, fathers' school involvement may simply be less visible than mothers' involvement. "The lower visibility of fathers at school might lead teachers and administrators to underestimate the interest of fathers and thus overlook them in designing parental involvement opportunities" (Shumow & Miller, 2001, p. 85).

Regardless, school librarians can work to reach out to less-involved parents, making the school library a comfortable and inviting place for them and consequently aligning it with family values and beliefs about what is important in their children's lives. While an intense level of family collaboration is not always practical for school librarians and is not always necessary for all students, reaching out to the home can reap positive benefits when students are having particular difficulty succeeding in school. At the most basic level, family collaboration can be encouraged by ensuring that the school library is inviting to families, that they feel welcome to stop in whenever they are in the school, and that they understand how they can contribute to the success of the school library in ways that are meaningful and worthwhile. Ample and interesting information about the school library could be made available through a newsletter or special posting to families on the school library Web site. As a rule, families will be most interested and involved when their children's work and contributions are showcased in the school library—including celebrations of students' reading and writing, displays of their artwork, or photographs of their performances or activities. As an easy example, when students' pictures or their writing is featured in the newsletter, families are far more interested in reading it and discussing it with their students.

WHAT YOU CAN DO

The unique character of the school library can mean that communication with parents does not occur as automatically as it does for classroom teachers, who routinely meet in parent–teacher conferences or exchange notes with parents. Nevertheless, frequent and effective partnerships can be fostered between the school libraries and families, and these partnerships can play important roles in enlisting families in strengthening their children's school success. Appropriate strategies will differ depending on a particular school's history, community, grade level, and resources, but one or more of the following strategies may be appropriate:

- Ideally, the school library should have a **Library Advisory Committee** (Shumow & Miller, 2001). This serves two purposes. It provides the school librarian with input from the community to help develop policies and procedures that are family-friendly and resonate with community values and goals, and it creates opportunities to educate community members about the role and function of the school library in the school. Obviously, teachers and administrators should be members of this committee, but in addition, one or more parents should be persuaded to volunteer. These volunteers can be the center's ambassadors into the community of parents and will strengthen the relationship with students' homes. By tracking the number of parents who are willing to serve in this capacity, it is possible to assess the success of the school library's alliances with families. A second way to assess these alliances is to track the attendance of and contributions made by students' parents at the Library Advisory Committee. In some cases, important changes have been noted in the behavior of children whose parents serve on the Library Advisory Committee. They may come to the school library more often, may engage the school librarian in more conversations, and/or may behave better than they did before their parents joined the committee.

- During **parent–teacher conferences,** the school library should be open and available for parents to stop in, browse through the materials, and ask questions. Serving coffee and refreshments is a good way to attract parents into the school library. Also, a tasteful display of student work will appeal to parents, especially when it is accompanied by recent photos of the students at work. It is a good idea to include work from as many students as possible and to update the display for each parent–teacher conference. Enthusiastic marketing helps! In the weeks leading up to the parent–teacher conferences, talk about the displayed student work in glowing terms whenever the students are in the center so that students will be predisposed to tell their parents about the display, and an announcement should be on the school library Web page. When parents do stop in, visit with them about the school library program, and gather their suggestions for future interactions with the school library and its program. Simple records (observation or hash marks on a pad of paper) can measure the number of parents who actually come for refreshments or to view the displays. It is also useful to prepare a brief questionnaire to gauge parent knowledge of the current programs or to hand out a small flyer describing the school library and its programs. Informal conversation can also provide information about the parents' knowledge about or attitude toward the school library program. These conversations can provide additional insight about the students and thus lead to stronger relationships with them. For example, parents may talk about a family pet, and the school librarian can ask the student at a later date how the pet is doing.

- The **Parent–Teacher Association (PTA)** or the **Parent–Teacher Organization (PTO)** is another way for the school librarian to connect to parents. Attending the meetings and being active in the PTA/PTO enables the school librarian to become acquainted with the parents. Again, research shows that a positive relationship with the parents will help students be more resilient. By recording observations, it is possible to document the number of relationships developed with parents through the PTA/PTO, and information learned through specific encounters can provide important suggestions and input about the school library programs. Again, observations of the behavior and actions of students whose parents are active in the PTA/PTO might be used to document the effectiveness of this technique.

- Some school librarians have sponsored successful parent **book clubs.** After reading controversial books, Pat Scales (2001) invited parents to come to her library once a month to discuss the teen titles. This allowed parents to learn about contemporary teen books as well as explore strategies for talking with their teens about controversial topics. Or, a parent–student book club could engage students and their parents in reading books together and talking together about the insights that they have gained. Parent–student book clubs may be particularly effective with younger readers. The school librarian's role is to select intriguing and engaging books as the focus of these clubs and to prepare questions to start the discussion. As parents become more familiar with and comfortable with the club and with each other, the discussions may become more animated and involved. The effectiveness of book clubs and the value that parents and students place on them can be assessed through attendance records or observations of the discussion, including the number of people who participate and the type and depth of the comments. Alternatively, a brief questionnaire could ask for specific types of information or for input about the strengths and weaknesses of the club.

- While not as common for school librarians as for classroom teachers, it is also appropriate to **call, e-mail, or write a note to parents,** especially to praise a student. Too often, schools wait to contact parents until there is a problem, and parents automatically assume that a note home means that their child has misbehaved in some way. It can be especially beneficial (for both parent and student) to communicate something positive. Either a phone call or a note sent to the home (via postal mail or e-mail if possible) can be appropriate. The note or conversation should briefly describe the action and convey pleasure. Be sure to include your name and note that you are the school librarian. The ideal would be to do this for all students in the school, but what is possible for a classroom teacher with limited numbers of students is not always feasible for the school librarian who has contact with all students in the school. However, it might be possible to reach more parents by selecting groups of students for this type of contact. For example, a note might be sent home saying: "We are celebrating the second grade class's conclusion of a successful unit on community helpers with a display in the school library. Please join us in congratulating your child on this achievement." To document this type of activity, record all parents contacted, note the type of contact, and then note any subsequent observations of student behavior that seem to result from this contact.

- The school library should have a **Web page** that provides information about the school library program. This Web page can be used to post a monthly school library newsletter. Be sure to include information for parents on this site. For example, if parents are allowed to check out books from the school library, the newsletter would be a good place to give parents pertinent details like the length of time they can keep the book, types of materials they can check out, and the policy about overdue materials. Also, if the teachers commonly assign homework, the school library Web page can be a great place to provide homework help—links to Web sites, information about the assignments, or links to databases and software programs available through the school library that can help students do their homework and help parents help students with the homework. Direct observation and feedback from the parents can help you evaluate the impact of a newsletter. For example, how many parents check out materials? How many materials are check out? How often? How many materials are overdue or lost? Also, a counter can be added to the Web page to see how often people view the newsletter or the homework page. While it is impossible to know for sure how many of the hits are parents and how many are teachers or students, the counter would give a broad indication of interest. Sometimes it may be appropriate to write a survey asking parents what is helpful on the homework page, what isn't helpful, and other things they would like to see there.

Given experience in and knowledge of the school, the school librarian may identify other ways to make the home–school library connection. Additionally, it is probably not appropriate to start all of these activities at the same time. Instead, balance efforts to reach out to the home with all of the other activities necessary for administering a quality school library program.

PLANNING FOR RESILIENCE

In today's world, accountability is important and resources are scarce. Therefore, there will be times when the school librarian will need to document the effectiveness of a program started in the library. Also, information on a program's effectiveness is necessary when planning the allocation of limited resources in the school library program. Based on the information given in Chapter 2, the following template has been completed for one of the previous suggestions.

HOW CAN I FIND OUT?

I. **Scenario** (Here I describe the situation that is the issue; that I am worried about, etc.)

Recently, I started a book club for parents of my high school students. I need to know how that is working and whether or not I should continue or adapt it.

II. **Resilience Area and Activities:** (Here I decide which area of resilience to focus on and how to do that.)
Strengthening ties between the school library and the home.

III. **Question** (What is the main question(s) I need to answer to decide whether or not the technique I chose is enhancing resilience?)
Do parents feel the parent book club is worthwhile? Do they want changes?

IV. **Methodology** (How will I gather information to answer the question?)

A. **What information do I need to gather?**

1. What do I want to know?
How parents feel about the book club and how well it is working.

2. What information do I need to find that out?
The opinions and reactions of parents.

B. **How might I gather that information?**

1. Use **existing records** or information.
Not available in this case.

2. **Observe** what is happening.
This gives me actions, but not the thoughts and opinions of the parents.

3. **Gather information** from people directly.
This is the best way for me to learn what parents are thinking.

a. **Interview**
This would give me information, but it would also be time consuming.

b. **Questionnaire**
This is likely the best technique because I can do it for 10 minutes at the end of a meeting; doing it at the end of the meeting will increase response rate. I will have a written record of the input without having to write or transcribe answers; parents will have relative privacy to voice opinions.

c. **Test**
Not appropriate for this case.

d. **Assignment or Exercise**
Not appropriate for this case.

C. **Collect the data** (using the technique identified previously).

1. Devise the instrument to use to collect data.
I need to create a short questionnaire for the parents to fill out. For example:

1. What do you believe works well in the book club right now?

2. What would you like to see changed in the book club?

3. What is your opinion of the books we have been reading?

4. What effect has the book club had on your reading?

5. What effect has the book club had on your interactions with your teen?

6. What are advantages and disadvantages of asking parents and teens to discuss the books together? Would you prefer the joint parent and teen discussions to be held every meeting or only occasionally?

7. Why do you believe the book club should or should not continue?

8. Please feel free to share any other comments you wish to make.

2. Administer the instrument.
Decide when you want to administer the questionnaire.

V. **Data Analysis** (Now what do I do with all this information?)

A. **Numbers**
No numbers on the questionnaire.

B. **Observations**
No observations recorded for this project.

C. **Interviews and Questionnaires**

1. **Closed questions**
No closed questions on this questionnaire

2. **Open questions**

a. **Group into categories**
As I review the questionnaires, group answers into categories. For example, for the first question, one parent might say, "I have enjoyed a chance to learn about the books Kathy likes"; another parent might say, "I didn't realize what these books were about and now I understand some of what Jane is talking about." Those two responses could be put into the same category. Another parent may respond that the 7:00 P.M. meetings on Tuesday are perfect for his schedule. That would belong in another category.

b. **Identify trends**
Once I have grouped the answers for each question into categories and know how many responses are in each category, I can identify trends. For example, 10 out of 12 parents believe the book club has helped them communicate better with their teens.

VI. **What does this tell me about my original question?**

   After looking at my analysis of the responses, I need to determine what the questionnaire results tell me. Is the book club working well? What needs to be kept the same? What needs to be changed? How do the parents feel about having the teens join them?

VII. **Using the information.**

   A. How does this help me make decisions or better understand resilience in my school library?

   What have I learned? Does this book club help me connect to parents? Do the parents value this experience? Am I seeing an immediate effect on students? (It might not be possible to see an immediate effect. The impact of connections to the family on resilience take time to document.)

   B. Use the information to decide whether to continue the current activity, make changes to the current activity, or devise and implement a second activity.

   Based on the results of the questionnaire and other input (casual comments from parents and from the students of parents involved; my own observations during the book club sessions, etc.) decide whether to keep the book club sessions as they are, to change them, or to discontinue the book club.

   C. Share the information with students, teachers, and administrators.

   One of the best ways to share the results of my investigation would be through an article in the school library Web site newsletter. Also, in my regular report to the principal, discuss the results and what I plan to do now. I might have an opportunity to report my study to the PTA/PTO.

REFERENCES

Carter, R. S., & Wojtkiewicz, R. A. (2000). Parental involvement with adolescents' education: Do daughters or sons get more help? *Adolescence, 35*(137), 29–44.

Christenson, S. L., & Anderson, A. R. (2002). Commentary: The centrality of the learning for students' academic enabler skills. *School Psychology review, 31*(3), 378–394.

Christenson, S. L., & Reschly, A. L. (2010). Check and Connect: Enhancing school completion through student engagement. In B. Doll, W. Pfohl, & J. Yoon (Eds.), *Handbook of youth prevention science* (pp. 327–348). New York: Routledge.

Comer, J. P., Haynes, N. M., Joyner, E. T., & Ben-Avie, M. (1996). *Rallying the whole village: The Comer process for reforming education*. New York: Teachers College Press.

Hill, N. E., & Taylor, L. C. (2004). Parental school involvement and children's academic achievement: Pragmatics and issues. *Current Directions in Psychological Science, 13*(4), 161–164.

Scales, P. (2001). *Teaching banned books: 12 guides for young readers*. Chicago: American Library Association.

Shumow, L., & Miller, J.D. (2001). Parents' at-home and at-school academic involvement with young adolescents. *Journal of Early Adolescence, 21*(1), 68–91.

Sinclair, M.F., Christenson, S.L., Evelo, D.L., & Hurley, C.M. (1998). Dropout prevention for youth with disabilities: Efficacy of a sustained school engagement procedure. *Exceptional Children, 65,* 7–21.

9

Pedagogical Techniques to Support Resilience

There are established instructional techniques that also support student resilience. Cooperative learning, by definition, means that students will be working together on activities or assignments. Literature circles are designed so that students follow a proscribed procedure to discuss books they have read. Peer tutoring pairs students together to help each other learn or review class material. All of these techniques support the development of peer relationships, but they can also encourage other elements of resilience. For example, peer tutoring can enhance academic efficacy as paired students realize they can succeed together, and literature circles can strengthen students' self-control by teaching the steps toward focused discussion procedures. This chapter provides more information on these pedagogical techniques.

COOPERATIVE LEARNING

Many professionals believe that cooperative learning was a natural outcome of the one-room school house. Like these early schools, cooperative learning creates situations where students share with and learn from each other, enhancing the learning that occurs. However, it requires substantial time to create effective cooperative learning activities. Experienced educators often say that it takes as much time to prepare a cooperative learning activity for students as it does to prepare a "traditional" lecture.

Characteristics

Slavin (1990) has identified four characteristics of cooperative learning.

1. *Face-to-face interaction*—When working with students in the school library, face-to-face interaction is not difficult to arrange. Students can work together at tables in the library, or even arrange chairs in a circle. Space groups far enough apart so that students can work without visual or vocal interference from other working groups.
2. *Positive interdependence*—When designing a cooperative learning experience it is important to make sure that all students must contribute to the assigned outcome. By separating the assignment or activity into discrete tasks, each student can be given primary responsibility for an identified section. For

example, working in groups of three to create a PowerPoint presentation, all students could be expected to locate information to be included in the final presentation. Then, one student can be in charge of writing the content of each slide, one student could be responsible for visual elements on each slide, and one student could be assigned to merge these into the Power-Point presentation.

3. *Individual accountability*—In a seeming contradiction, each student in each group must be held accountable for participating in and contributing to the group's activities. This can often be the hardest part of creating cooperative learning experiences. One way to ensure student accountability is to assign each student a specific task, as described in the positive interdependence section. Another way is to have students turn in a confidential rating of all members of the group, including themselves. Students should be told in advance that they will be rating the participation of each group member at the end of the activity. Also, the school librarians should make very clear that they should be told immediately if one or more students are not contributing to the group's work. Students should know, in advance, that groups may be dissolved or reformed as needed. Any individual student who is removed from the group for cause must then complete the work individually. Alternatively, students who consistently do not contribute in a group could be grouped together, and they may learn to work instead of taking advantage of the work of others.

4. *Interpersonal and small-group skills*—Students do not automatically understand how to work in groups and must be taught how to function effectively in groups. Start slowly, with only 10 or 15 minutes of carefully designed cooperative activities. For example, when teaching third grade students to identify various genres of books, have each team of students spend 10 minutes classifying preselected sets of books that you have put on tables in the library. Working cooperatively on activities such as these will require that students have a rudimentary understanding of group dynamics. Students who understand how people work together in groups can be more effective working in a cooperative setting. Start by talking with students about different things that can happen in groups and how people have different functions in a group. Then, assign roles for the brief cooperative activities—for example, one student can be the discussion leader, another can make sure everyone has a chance to participate, another can take notes on the discussion, and one can be the time keeper. All students will need instruction in group dynamics if they are to be successful. There are even cooperative learning activities that help students learn to function in groups. For example, there is a lesson plan called "Traits Needed for Effective Group Process" that is available through the Educator's Reference Desk (Hill, 1994).

Cooperative Learning Strategies

There are a variety of specific cooperative learning strategies that can be used to direct students' work together. It is important to match the strategy to the characteristics of the material to be learned, to the activity or the assignment, and to the students who will participate. Also, some techniques will work better with certain students and classes than others.

Kagan (1994) describes numerous specific cooperative learning techniques that are appropriate for elementary, middle, or high school students. Six are discussed here.

1. **Brainstorming**—Brainstorming is a good technique to open a unit of study or to generate a list of items for future work. For example, when teaching students how to use an OPAC and find books on a specific subject, brainstorming can be used to gather students' suggestions of words to use in a search of the OPAC. Rules for brainstorming are that all suggestions are equally appropriate and that students are not allowed to belittle or criticize suggestions from other students.

2. **Mini lecture**—Sometimes the best, most effective way to convey information to students is to use a brief lecture. In most cases, no more than 10 to 15 minutes will be needed to briefly present the information students need for subsequent activities. A handout or worksheet can then reinforce your comments and help students remember what you said.

3. **Roundtable technique**—This is similar to but more structured than brainstorming. After a question is raised, a pad of paper is passed around the group. Each person writes down a response that is different from the other responses already recorded. Decide in advance whether or not each person has to write a response and whether others in the group can give help. In the school library, for example, this technique might be used to remind students of the variety of resources available. The initial question might be, "Where could I find information about rocks and minerals?" Answers could include: books, magazines, DVD, mineral specimens, Web sites, encyclopedias, or people.

4. **Send-a-problem problem solving**—For this technique, a separate envelope is prepared for each problem that will be solved. Each group receives one envelope that has a description of the problem written on the outside. The group writes down possible solutions, puts their answers in the envelope, and passes the envelope to the next team. When receiving an envelope, the next team may not look at the responses already in the envelope, but instead generates their own solutions. When the envelopes return to the original teams, all of the suggested solutions are reviewed and compiled into one statement. The send-a-problem technique usually works best with three to four groups, with three to four students in each group. For example, after teaching high school students about plagiarism, the send-a-problem scenarios could describe real-world situations involving plagiarism and ask students what they would do in each case.

5. **Talking chips**—This technique helps to ensure that all students participate in a discussion. Each student in the group receives a chip (or other token), and the group receives a topic for discussion. Each group member "spends" a chip to make a comment or response. That student may not make any other comments until all other group members have "spent"

their chip, too. Then, if time permits, the chips are redistributed and the discussion continues. For example, in a discussion of an assigned book, students could be asked to make one positive comment about the main character, and then name one thing they did not like about the main character. In this case, using chips would help ensure that all students are contributing to the discussion and that one or two students do not dominate the group.

6. **Three-step interview**—This technique helps students learn from each other. Students are assigned to groups of four. Within each group, pairs of students interview each other. Then, each student shares the information gained through the interview with the other students. For example, if eighth grade students have researched a prominent American, the three-step interview would be one way for students to learn each other's person. Prepared questions (Who is your person? Why is your person famous? What was the most interesting thing you found out about your person?) can be used for students to interview each other. Then, students who conducted an interview will explain what they learned from their partner. (The students who actually did the research are not allowed to share their own discoveries.)

Forming Groups

In cooperative learning, students work in groups. It is important to make decisions about group membership during the instructional design stage instead of trying to organize student groups after the lesson has begun. There are several factors to be considered (Miller, 1988). The size of each group should be decided in advance. Usually, three to four students per group is ideal. This group size is small enough that each student will participate and large enough that different ideas or skills are available to the group. Sometimes, however, it is useful to put the students in pairs, which almost always ensures each student is active in the group activity.

Also, it is important to decide how students will become members of a particular group. In some cases, it is good to let students self-select their fellow group members. This allows those students who already know each other to strengthen their relationship. However, student selection can be very discouraging for students who are not chosen by anyone. Whenever classes have one or more neglected students, it is best to assign groups rather than allowing students to choose their groups.

Assign students to groups before the lesson begins. Advanced formation of the groups can be based on knowledge of each student and the skills and knowledge that students will contribute to the group. For example, when students are preparing a group report on a country and creating country posters to display in the school library, the group will need at least one student who is a good reader, one who is artistic, one who is good at searching for information, and one who can compose the text for the poster.

Finally, students can be grouped randomly. Each table in the school library could have a number and a set of materials for the upcoming activity. Students can draw numbers as they come into the library and go to the corresponding table and begin work. The school librarian should circulate while the groups are working to supervise, provide assistance as needed, and to give support.

Some student groups will be used for only one activity. Others may endure over the course of a week, month, semester, or school year. The term of the group assignment depends, in part, on the nature of the task and the amount of effort and time required to complete the activity. Students may belong to several groups simultaneously and do not necessarily need to work with the same group of students for all group work in the school library.

Value of Cooperative Learning

Both formal research and informal anecdotal evidence indicate that cooperative learning has positive benefits for students. One study succinctly reports the results:

> *Between November and January, students . . . felt more responsible for ensuring that all group members learned the assigned material, perceived more resource interdependence among students, felt more encouragement to learn and more concern about one's learning from peers, perceived the students within the class as being friends and as liking to work with each other, and felt less alienated from school and classmates.* (Johnson, Johnson, Buckman, & Richards, 1985, p. 410)

LITERATURE CIRCLES

Students participating in a literature circle have all read the same book and engage in a structured discussion of that book. Discussions may focus on the literary elements of the books (such as plot, style, theme, or character), issues raised by the books (such as relationships with peers or parents), or focus on content (such as whether or not scientific method has been accurately portrayed in a biography of Curie). The discussion questions can be developed in advance or drawn from activities related to the books. The school librarian can write the questions, or the students may write the questions based on their understanding of the book.

Generally, students in a literature circle volunteer for or are assigned specific roles for the discussion. These roles may include leader, recorder, devil's advocate, literary critic, or connector. Fink's (n.d.) Web site lists four specific roles and provides job descriptions and worksheets to help students prepare for the literature circle discussion.

As with other forms of cooperative learning, students will not automatically know how to participate in a literature circle without instruction from the school librarian. It can be helpful to first conduct literature circle style discussions with the whole class, then break the class into smaller groups and use adult-constructed questions to guide the discussion. With time and practice, students will be able to prepare their own questions and independently direct their own participation in literature discussions.

The Web sites by the College of Education, Daniels, Fink, and Noe and Johnson (listed in the Resources section) can provide useful and information and guidance in the use of literature circles with students in kindergarten through twelfth grade.

PEER TUTORING

In peer tutoring situations, students help each other to learn and learn by teaching each other (Gartner & Reissman, 1993). As with other forms of cooperative learning, the school librarian should decide how to pair students before the lesson begins. It can be effective to pair students in advance, or to allow students to spontaneously form groups when it is time for them to work together. Also, both students can take turns being the tutor, instead of always having a more proficient student tutor a less proficient student. According to Gartner and Reisman (1993), "The critical importance of youth having the opportunity to participate in meaningful roles such as youth-helping-youth is a salient factor in preventing social problems, including substance abuse, teen pregnancy, and delinquency. The need exists to expand the opportunity to have all students experience the helping role" (p. 20). The researchers note it is important to provide students with training on how to serve as a tutor.

An important development is Class Wide Peer Tutoring (CWPT), developed by Greenwood, Delquadri, and Carta (1997) for grades one through eight. CWPT pairs students for a week, and they work together on reading, math, or another subject to provide opportunity for practice and quizzing and immediate feedback. Points are awarded to both the tutee and the tutor, and a test on Friday assesses progress made during the week. Another option is to divide the class into two teams of paired students, and competition is based on points awarded and test scores. Greenwood et al.'s (1997) manual *Together We Can!* provides ample detail for educators who with to implement the program.

In the school library, CWPT could be used when teaching the Dewey Decimal system, Web site evaluation, or any other topic where students need practice and feedback. Awarding points and testing help to create a gaming type atmosphere, which may or may not be desirable, depending on the social dynamics in your school.

ADDITIONAL RESOURCES

The following resources will provide more information on cooperative learning, literature circles, and peer tutoring. There are also other methods you can use to help students work together. No one method is appropriate for all children, and no one method will work in every school. It is important to select one or more methods that work for your students and teachers.

College of Education. (2007). *Overview of literature circles.* Seattle, WA: Seattle University. Retrieved June 4, 2009, from: http://www.litcircles.org/Overview/overview.html.
   This overview briefly talks about the goals, timelines, scheduling, choosing books, forming groups, reading and preparing for discussion, the discussion itself, written products, responses, focus lessons, extension projects, and assessment and evaluation for literature circles. Additional pages on the Web site provide extensive information and focus on kindergarten through eighth grades.

Daniels, H. (2002). *Literature circles: Voice and choice in book clubs and reading groups* (chapter 1). Portland, ME: Stenhouse Publishers. Retrieved June 4, 2009, from: http://www.literature circles.com/article1.htm.
   This is a good introduction to and overview of literature circles. It cautions against using the role sheets rigorously throughout the course of the year. Instead, use them to help stu-

dents understand the various roles possible, and then wean students away from them to enable less mechanical discussions to occur.

Farmer, L.S.J. (1999). *Cooperative learning activities in the library media center.* Englewood, CO: Libraries Unlimited.
This book has chapters on the nature of cooperative learning, inclusive ways of learning, outcomes-based education, information literacy, building a learning community, and activity plans for a wide range of subjects.

Fink, L.S. (n.d.). *Literature circles: Getting started.* Retrieved June 4, 2009, from: http://www.read writethink.org/lessons/lesson_view.asp?id=19 (A National Council of Teachers of English sponsored site.)
This site does a nice job of outlining how to introduce literature circles to students and includes detailed lesson plans for teaching about group work, demonstrating each role, and gradually transferring responsibility for guiding discussions to the students.

Fogarty, R. (1990). *Designs for cooperative interactions.* Arlington Heights, IL: Skylight Professional Development.
Several cooperative learning models are presented, following a brief introduction to cooperative learning. This book includes cooperative learning techniques such as tell-retell and paired partners.

Gibbs, J. (1995). *Tribes: A new way of learning and being together.* Sausalito, CA: Center Source.
The general idea behind this book is to have all children feel included, and it includes elements of cooperative learning and lots of suggested activities.

Greenwood, C.R., Delquadri, J.C., & Carta, J.J. (1997). *Together we can! Class wide peer tutoring to improve basic academic skills.* Longmont, CO: Sopris West.
This book describes the process for Class Wide Peer Tutoring with lots of tips and examples.

Kagan, S. (1992). *Cooperative learning.* San Juan Capistrano, CA: Kagan Cooperative Learning.
Kagan's book provides an in-depth exploration of the theory of cooperative learning and includes multiple techniques to use in the classroom.

Karns, M. (1994). *How to create positive relationships with students: A handbook of group activities and teaching strategies.* Champaign, IL: Research Press.
This book does a very nice job of suggesting specific ways to reach out to students; one strategy recommended is active learning.

Noe, K.L.S., & Johnson, N.J. (1999). *Getting started with literature circles.* Norwood, MA: Christopher-Gordon Publishers.
Gives an overview of cooperative learning, including information on implementation and teaching social skills. See, in particular, "Planning for Literature Circles," adapted from chapter 3 of this book. Retrieved June 4, 2009, from: http://www.litcircles.org/Structure/planning.html. Good information about the differences between the "ideal" (i.e., what is in the literature) and the "real" (what really happens as you work through literature circles in the classroom with students).

Wright, J. (2004). *Kids as reading helpers: A peer tutor training manual.* Retrieved June 4, 2009, from: http://www.jimwrightonline.com/pdfdocs/prtutor/peerTutorManual.pdf
This 64-page training manual starts with a rationale for peer tutoring, then addresses preparation, launching, and monitoring a peer tutoring program.

REFERENCES

Fink, L.S. (n.d.). *Literature circles: getting started.* Retrieved June 4, 2009, from: http://www.read writethink.org/lessons/lesson_view.asp?id=19.

Gartner, A., & Riessman, F. (1993). Peer-tutoring: Toward a new model. ERIC Identifier: ED362506 Washington, DC: ERIC Clearinghouse on Teaching and Teacher Education. Available at: http://www.ericdigests.org/1994/peer.htm.

Greenwood, C.R., Delquadri, J.C., & Carta, J.J. (1997). *Together we can! Class wide peer tutoring to improve basic academic skills.* Longmont, CO: Sopris West.

Hill, M. (1994). Traits needed for effective group process. In *Educator's Reference Desk.* Retrieved May 31, 2009, from: http://www.eduref.org/cgi-bin/printlessons.cgi/Virtual/Lessons/ Interdisciplinary/INT0074.html.

Johnson, D.W., Johnson, R.T., Buckman, L.A., & Richards, P.S. (1985). The effect of prolonged implementation of cooperative learning on social support within the classroom. *Journal of Psychology, 119*(5), 405–411.

Kagan, S. (1994). *Cooperative learning.* San Jan Capistrano, CA: Kagan Cooperative Learning.

Miller, E.S. (1988). *Considerations in forming groups.* Howard County Staff Development Center.

Slavin, R.E. (1990). *Cooperative learning: Theory, research, and practice.* Englewood Cliffs, NJ: Prentice Hall.

Appendix A

Template for Planning for Resilience

HOW CAN I FIND OUT?

   I. **Scenario** (Here I describe the situation that is the issue that I am worried about, etc.)

  II. **Resilience Area and Activities** (Here I decide which area of resilience to focus on and how to do that.)

 III. **Question** (What is the main question I need to answer to decide whether or not the technique I chose is enhancing resilience?)

 IV. **Methodology** (How will I gather information to answer the question?)

    A. What information do I need to gather?

    B. How might I gather that information?

      1. Use **existing records** or information.

      2. **Observe** what is happening.

      3. **Gather information** from people directly.

        a. Interview

        b. Questionnaire

        c. Test

        d. Assignment or Exercise

    C. **Collect the data** (using the technique I identified previously).

  V. **Data Analysis** (Now what do I do with all this information?)

    A. **Numbers**

      1. Frequencies

      2. Bar graphs

        3. Percentages

        4. Pie graph

        5. Change over time

    B. **Observations**

        1. Group into categories

        2. Charts or graphs

    C. **Interviews and Questionnaires**

        1. Closed questions

        2. Open questions

            a. Group into categories

            b. Identify trends

VI. **What does this tell me about my original question?**

VII. **Using the information.**

    A. How does this help me make decisions or better understand resilience in my school library?

    B. Use the information to decide whether to continue the current activity, make changes to the current activity, or devise and implement another activity.

    C. Share the information with students, teachers, and administrators.

Appendix B

Resilience and *Standards for the 21st-Century Learner*

INTRODUCTION

In 2007, the American Association of School Librarians (AASL) released *Standards for the 21st-Century Learner*. Five common beliefs provide the context for the standards themselves. These five beliefs are:

- Reading is a window to the world.
- Inquiry provides a framework for learning.
- Ethical behavior in the use of information must be taught.
- Technology skills are crucial for future employment needs.
- Equitable access is a key component for education.

Within this broad framework, four additional common beliefs are identified to guide implementation of the standards. Students use skills, resources, and tools to:

- Inquire, think critically, and gain knowledge.
- Draw conclusions, make informed decisions, apply knowledge to new situations, and create new knowledge.
- Share knowledge and participate ethically and productively as members of our democratic society.
- Pursue personal and aesthetic growth.

Then each of these four goals has four subsections: skills, dispositions in action, responsibilities, and self-assessment strategies.

REACTION TO THE NEW STANDARDS

Since their introduction, the standards have been widely discussion in the school library community. As Taylor (2008) notes, "[The new standards] are meant to get us library media specialists to think differently about how we interact with classroom teachers, develop our curriculum, and provide instruction. Yet, the mission of the standards remains the same—to have staff and students become better users of information" (p. 24).

It is also important to realize that the new standards are validated by research being done around the world. Mardis's (2008) article shows how each of the four overall goals are supported by solid research studies in a variety of places, including the United States, England, or Greece. She concludes: "Library media specialists, technology specialists, teachers, school administrators, and community members have articulated guidelines that assure the same progressive and exciting future for our children. For library media specialists, the *Standards* not only represent a change, but also an unprecedented opportunity to support all education stakeholders with common goals for students and schools" (p. 58).

THE ROLE OF RESILIENCE

Close reading and analysis of *Standards for the 21st-Century Learning* shows that many of the techniques to enhance resilience presented in this book can also enhance and support these new standards. Self-selected learning goals, academic efficacy, and peer relationships are closely allied with these new standards.

Self-Selected Learning Goals (SSLG)

Self-Selected Learning Goals is the element of resilience that is most obvious in the new *Standards for the 21st-Century Learner*. Each of the standards includes a section on self-assessment strategies, which match resilient elements within the self-selected learning goals. For example, one element from each section of the AASL standards is matched with a specific segment of the Self-Selected Learning Goals (SSLG) chapter below:

1.2.5 Demonstrate adaptability by changing the inquiry focus, questions, resources, or strategies when necessary to achieve success.
SSLG . . . planfully altering their behavior in ways that increase their likelihood of reaching their goal. (p. 3, chap. 5)

2.4.2 Reflect on systematic process, and assess for completeness of investigation.
SSLG [Self-selected learning] goals also contribute to students persistence when learning because they define the end point of a learning task. (p. 2, chap. 5)

3.4.2 Assess the quality and effectiveness of the learning product.
SSLG Among the skills that foster students ability to work independently is: "Judging the quality of [the] work." (p. 7, chap. 5)

4.4.3 Recognize how to focus efforts in personal learning.
SSLG Another skill that fosters students ability to work independently is: analyzing tasks and determining appropriate strategies to accomplish them. (p. 6, chap. 5)

As shown with the four previous examples, there is a close relationship between self-selected learning goals and the self-assessment strategies of the new standards.

Peer Relationships

The third overall goal for the *Standards* states: "Students will use skills, resources and tools to share knowledge and participate ethically and productively as members of our democratic society." Then, there are numerous references throughout the *Standards* that use terminology such as:

- collaborate with others
- contribute to the exchange of ideas
- use interaction with and feedback from
- sharing
- participating actively with others
- demonstrate teamwork

Overall, this implies that students need to have good working relationships with their fellow students.

One of the important elements of resilience is that students need comfortable relationships with their peers. Therefore, any work done to support or improve strong peer relationships also supports the new *Standards*.

Academic Efficacy

The relationship between the *Standards* and resilience as presented in this book is less obvious for academic efficacy, but it is still present. For example, each of the following points from the *Standards* actually relates to academic efficacy:

1.2.2   Demonstrates confidence and self direction by making independent choices in the selection of resources and information.
4.3.3   Seek opportunities for pursuing personal and aesthetic growth.

Those students who demonstrate academic efficacy will probably be successful in several ways identified in the new *Standards*.

CONCLUSION

The new *Standards for the 21st-Century Learner* are significantly different from former information literacy standards. These are good changes that align with standards from other educational groups, and they will truly help us move forward as we work with students. Also, the elements of resilience presented in this book will support many efforts to enable students to become the information literate citizens of tomorrow.

REFERENCES

American Association of School Librarians. (2007). *Standards for the 21st Century Learner.* Chicago: American Library Association. Retrieved September 7, 2009, from: http://www.ala.org/aasl/standards.

Mardis, M. A. (2008). Thirty Helens agree: 2007 research supports AASL's *Standards for the 21st-Century Learner. School Library Media Activities Monthly, 24*(10), 56–58.

Taylor, J. (2008). Transforming literacy: The new standards. *School Library Media Activities Monthly, 25*(4), 24–26.

Appendix C

ClassMaps Survey 2007 for School Libraries

Directions: These questions ask what is true about *students in the school library.* For each question, circle the choice that is true for you. Do not put your name on the paper. No one will know what your answers are.

I am a: ☐ BOY / MALE ☐ GIRL / FEMALE I am in the ＿＿grade.

Believing in Me

1. I know how to find information and books in the school library.

NEVER   SOMETIMES   OFTEN   ALMOST ALWAYS

2. I can do as well as most kids in using the school library.

NEVER   SOMETIMES   OFTEN   ALMOST ALWAYS

3. I can help other kids understand how to use the school library.

NEVER   SOMETIMES   OFTEN   ALMOST ALWAYS

4. I can be a very good student in the school library.

NEVER   SOMETIMES   OFTEN   ALMOST ALWAYS

5. I can do the hard work in the school library.

NEVER   SOMETIMES   OFTEN   ALMOST ALWAYS

6. I expect to do very well when I work hard in the school library.

NEVER   SOMETIMES   OFTEN   ALMOST ALWAYS

My School Librarian

7. My school librarian listens carefully to me when I talk.

NEVER   SOMETIMES   OFTEN   ALMOST ALWAYS

8. My school librarian helps me when I need help.

NEVER   SOMETIMES   OFTEN   ALMOST ALWAYS

My School Librarian

9. My school librarian respects me.

NEVER   SOMETIMES   OFTEN   ALMOST ALWAYS

10. My school librarian likes having me in the school library.

NEVER   SOMETIMES   OFTEN   ALMOST ALWAYS

11. My school librarian makes it fun to be in the school library.

NEVER   SOMETIMES   OFTEN   ALMOST ALWAYS

12. My school librarian thinks I do a good job on work in the school library.

NEVER   SOMETIMES   OFTEN   ALMOST ALWAYS

13. My school librarian is fair to me.

NEVER   SOMETIMES   OFTEN   ALMOST ALWAYS

Taking Charge

14. I want to know more about the things we learn in the school library.

NEVER   SOMETIMES   OFTEN   ALMOST ALWAYS

15. I work as hard as I can in the school library.

NEVER   SOMETIMES   OFTEN   ALMOST ALWAYS

16. I learn because I want to and not just because the school librarian tells me to.

NEVER   SOMETIMES   OFTEN   ALMOST ALWAYS

17. When the work is hard in the school library, I keep trying until I figure it out.

NEVER   SOMETIMES   OFTEN   ALMOST ALWAYS

18. I know the things I learn in the school library will help me outside of school.

NEVER   SOMETIMES   OFTEN   ALMOST ALWAYS

19. I can tell when I make a mistake on my work in the school library.

NEVER   SOMETIMES   OFTEN   ALMOST ALWAYS

My Classmates

20. I have a lot of fun with my friends in the school library.

NEVER   SOMETIMES   OFTEN   ALMOST ALWAYS

21. My friends care about me a lot.

NEVER   SOMETIMES   OFTEN   ALMOST ALWAYS

22. I have friends to eat lunch with and play with at recess.

NEVER   SOMETIMES   OFTEN   ALMOST ALWAYS

23. I have friends that like me the way I am.

NEVER   SOMETIMES   OFTEN   ALMOST ALWAYS

24. My friends like me as much as they like other kids.

NEVER   SOMETIMES   OFTEN   ALMOST ALWAYS

25. I have friends who will stick up for me if someone picks on me.

NEVER   SOMETIMES   OFTEN   ALMOST ALWAYS

Following the Class Rules

26. Most kids work quietly and calmly in the school library.

NEVER   SOMETIMES   OFTEN   ALMOST ALWAYS

Following the Class Rules

27. Most kids in the school library listen carefully when the librarian gives directions.

NEVER   SOMETIMES   OFTEN   ALMOST ALWAYS

28. Most kids follow the rules in the school library.

NEVER   SOMETIMES   OFTEN   ALMOST ALWAYS

29. Most kids in the school library pay attention when they are supposed to.

NEVER   SOMETIMES   OFTEN   ALMOST ALWAYS

30. Most kids do their work when they are supposed to in the school library.

NEVER   SOMETIMES   OFTEN   ALMOST ALWAYS

31. Most kids in this class behave well even when the school librarian isn't watching.

NEVER   SOMETIMES   OFTEN   ALMOST ALWAYS

Talking With My Parents

32. My parents and I talk about what I am learning in the school library.

NEVER   SOMETIMES   OFTEN   ALMOST ALWAYS

33. My parents and I talk about ways that I can do well in school.

NEVER   SOMETIMES   OFTEN   ALMOST ALWAYS

34. My parents and I talk about good things I have done in the school library

NEVER   SOMETIMES   OFTEN   ALMOST ALWAYS

35. My parents and I talk about problems I have in the school library.

NEVER   SOMETIMES   OFTEN   ALMOST ALWAYS

I worry that. . . .

36. I worry that other kids will do mean things to me.

NEVER   SOMETIMES   OFTEN   ALMOST ALWAYS

37. I worry that other kids will tell lies about me.

NEVER   SOMETIMES   OFTEN   ALMOST ALWAYS

38. I worry that other kids will hurt me on purpose.

NEVER   SOMETIMES   OFTEN   ALMOST ALWAYS

39. I worry that other kids will say mean things about me.

NEVER   SOMETIMES   OFTEN   ALMOST ALWAYS

40. I worry that other kids will leave me out on purpose.

NEVER   SOMETIMES   OFTEN   ALMOST ALWAYS

41. I worry that other kids will try to make my friends stop liking me.

NEVER   SOMETIMES   OFTEN   ALMOST ALWAYS

42. I worry that other kids will make me do things I don't want to do.

NEVER   SOMETIMES   OFTEN   ALMOST ALWAYS

43. I worry that other kids will take things away from me.

NEVER   SOMETIMES   OFTEN   ALMOST ALWAYS

Kids In This Class

44. Kids argue a lot with each other when we are in the school library.

NEVER   SOMETIMES   OFTEN   ALMOST ALWAYS

Kids In This Class

45. Kids pick on or make fun of each other when we are in the school library.

NEVER   SOMETIMES   OFTEN   ALMOST ALWAYS

46. Kids tease each other or call each other names when we are in the school library.

NEVER   SOMETIMES   OFTEN   ALMOST ALWAYS

47. Kids hit or push each other when we are in the school library.

NEVER   SOMETIMES   OFTEN   ALMOST ALWAYS

48. Kids bad things about each other when we are in the school library.

NEVER   SOMETIMES   OFTEN   ALMOST ALWAYS

Index

ABC (antecedents, behaviors, consequences) framework (for behavioral control), 53

Academic efficacy: formation of, 24–26; learning environment changes, 29; motivation strategies, 27–29; planning for resilience, 29–35, 30–35; school effectiveness and, 9, 23–35; self-instruction strategies, 26–27

Adolescents: behavioral self-control of, 47–62; caring relationships with teachers, 63–74; parental education and success of, 93; parental involvement and success of, 92; relationships with peers, 77–88; risk conditions/outcomes, 2. *See also* Children; Students

Adult-managed behavioral control strategies, 47–62; classroom meetings, 51; core of program, 48; individual student behavior plans, 56–57; internalized speech strategy, 51–52; interpersonal cognitive problem solving, 52; negative consequences, 50–51; planning for resilience, 57–62; positive consequences or rewards, 49–50; reciprocal peer tutoring, 55–56; rules, 48–49; self-modification, 53–55; simplified self-monitoring, 55; teaching effective routines, 52–53

Adults: behavior-control management by, 48–51; bullying intervention, 79–81; checklist contribution by, 40; contributions to academic efficacy, 24–25; cues to students by, 52; meeting with other adults, 19–20; nonjudgmental attitude by, 29; as positive role models, 25; risk conditions in, 2; rules reinforcement by, 65; strong relationships with children, 9; student friendships encouraged by, 77–78; ten commandments for, 68; value of nurturing by, 3. *See also* School librarians; Teachers

Adults, strong relationships with, 9

Anderson, A. R., 4

Area and activities focus determination step (in resilience plan), 9

Assor, A., 64

Australia resilience studies, 1–2

Bandura, Albert, 23

Bar graphs: behavioral self-control example, 59–60; caring/authentic relationships example, 72; ClassMaps Surveys example, 32; described, 15; role of peer relationships example, 85; self-selected learning goals example, 32

Bear, G. C., 48

Behavioral self-control (resilience characteristic). *See* Adult-managed behavioral control strategies

Behavior plans (for individual students), 56–57

Ben-Avie, M., 91

Book clubs, 9–10, 81, 95

Brainstorming technique (cooperative learning), 103

Bullying intervention, 77, 79–81

Caring/authentic relationships between teachers and students strategies, 63–74; fostering relevance, 65–66; high emotional support strategies, 65; high expectations of students, 66; instructional excellence by teachers, 64; instructional support strategies, 65; planning for resilience, 69–74; respectfulness, 63–64; suppression of criticism, 66

Carta, J. J., 106

Change over time, 17

Check and Connect program (for disengaged students), 91–92

Children: behavioral self-control of, 47–62; caring relationships with teachers, 63–74; effectiveness evaluation for, 10, 19–20; importance of adults for, 24; relationships with peers, 77–88; resilience characteristics/studies, 1–3; school's effectiveness for, 3–4;

teaching steps for small vs. older, 29. *See also* Adolescents; Students
Christenson, S. L., 4
ClassMaps Survey for School Libraries, 20–21, 31, 32, 70, 88, 115–18
Classroom meetings, 51
Class Wide Peer Tutoring (CWPT), 107
Closed questions, 18–19
Comer, J. P., 91
Consequences for behavioral self-control, 49–51
Cooperative learning, 8, 82; characteristics, 101–2; definition, 101; group formation, 104–5; strategies/techniques, 102–4; value of, 105

Data analysis step (in resilience plan): for academic efficacy, 31; for behavioral self-control, 59; for caring/authentic relationships, 71–74; interviews and questionnaires, 18–20; numbers, 14–17; observations, 17–18; for role of family, 98; for role of peer relationships, 84–88; for self-selected learning goals, 44
Delquadri, J. C., 106

Epstein, J., 65
Extracurricular activities, 81

Facilities (physical setting), 80–81
Families, engagement with schools, 9, 91–99; book clubs, 95; calling, email, note to parents, 95–96; characteristics of less-involved parents, 92–93; fathers' vs. mothers' involvement, 93; Library Advisory Committee involvement, 94; Parent-Teacher Association/Parent-Teacher Organization, 95; parent-teacher conferences, 94–95; planning for resilience, 96–99; resilience in, 3; school Web page, 96; support of classroom learning by, 4
Fantuzzo, J. W., 55
Focus determination/area and activities: for academic efficacy, 30; for behavioral self-control, 57; for caring/authentic relationships, 69; described, 9; for role of family, 97; for role of peer relationships, 83; for self-selected learning goals, 42
Formal evaluation of resilience plans, 7
Frequencies: behavioral self-control example, 59; caring/authentic relationships example, 71; described, 14–15; plan template example, 18; role of peer relationships example, 85; self-selected learning goals example, 43, 44
Friendships: adult promotion of continuation of, 78; as basis for effective schools, 3; bullying

and, 79; extracurricular activities and, 81; identification of, 77. *See also* Peer relationship development strategies

Gartner, A., 106
Goal setting for students, 38–39
Great Britain resilience studies, 1–2
Greenwood, C. R., 106

Hamre, B. K., 64
Haynes, N. M., 91
High-risk children. *See* Children

Internalized speech strategy (for student behavioral control), 51–52
Interpersonal cognitive problem solving (for student behavioral control), 52
Interviews and questionnaires components (of data analysis): closed questions, 18–19; open questions, 19–20

Joyner, E. T., 91

Kagan, S., 103
Kaplan, H., 64
Karns, M., 67
Kitsantas, A., 37

Learning environment structure, 29
Learning strategies for students, 26–29
Li, L., 47
Library Advisory Committee, 94
Literature circles, 8, 83–85, 87–88, 102, 106

Methodology (for resilience plan), information gathering plan, 10–14; for academic efficacy, 30–31; assignments/exercises, 13–14; for behavioral control, 58; for caring/authentic relationships, 70; data collection, 14; existing records, 11; interviews, 11–12; observation, 11; questionnaires, 12–13; for role of family, 97; for role of peer relationships, 84; for self-selected learning goals, 42–43; tests, 13
Mini-lecture technique (cooperative learning), 103
Motivation strategies, for students, 27–29

Negative consequences for lack of behavioral self-control, 50
Numbers component (of data analysis): bar graphs, 15; change over time, 17; frequencies, 14–15; percentages, 15–16; pie graphs, 16–17

Observations component (of data analysis): cat-
egory grouping, 17–18; charts or graphs, 18
Open questions, 19–20
Outcomes analysis (of resilience plan), 20

Parent-Teacher Association (PTA), 95
Parent-teacher conferences, 94–95
Parent-Teacher Organization (PTO), 95
Pedagogical techniques for supporting resilience, 101–6; cooperative learning, 8, 82,
101–5; literature circles, 8, 83–85, 87–88, 102,
106; peer tutoring, 55–56, 82–83, 101, 107
Peer relationship development strategies, 9,
77–88; book clubs, 81; cooperative learning,
82; extracurricular activities, 81; literature
circles, 83; physical settings, 80–81; planning
for resilience, 83–88; strategies for promoting, 8, 9; support of peers, 81–82; tutoring by
peers, 82–83
Peer tutoring, 82–83; benefits of, 101; Class Wide
Peer Tutoring, 107; Reciprocal Peer Tutoring,
55–56; role of school librarian, 107
Percentages: behavioral self-control example,
59; caring/authentic relationships example,
71; description, 15–16; in pie graphs, 16–17;
planning template example, 18; role of peer
relationships example, 88; self-selected
learning goals example, 44
Persuasion, for academic efficacy, 24–25
Peterson, L., 47
Pianta, R. C., 64
Pie graphs: in behavioral self-control example,
59–60; caring/authentic relationship example, 73; description, 16–17, 16–18; role
of peer relationships example, 89; in self-
selected learning example, 44; template example, 18
Planning for resilience: for academic efficacy,
30–35; for behavioral self-control, 57–62; for
caring/authentic student-teacher relationships, 69–74; for families, 96–99; for peer
relationships, 83–88; plan template, 109–10;
for self-selected learning goals, 42–45
Positive consequences for behavioral self-
control, 49–50

Question determination step (in resilience plan):
for academic efficacy, 30, 33; for behavioral
self-control, 58; for caring/authentic relationships, 69, 73; explained, 9–10; for role of family, 97; for role of peer relationships, 83; for
self-selected learning goals, 42; types of, 17, 18

Reciprocal Peer Tutoring (RPT) strategy, 55–56
Reisman, F., 106
Relationships between teachers and students.
See Caring/authentic relationships between
teachers and students
Resilience: defined, 1–3; six characteristics of, 9
Resilience plans, effectivness evaluations, 7–21;
ClassMap Survey for School Libraries,
20–21, 31, 32, 70, 88, 115–18; planning tem-
plate, 8–20; targeting/method decisions, 8;
types of, 7
Rewards for behavioral self-control, 49–51
Ridley, D. S., 47
Rohrbeck, C. A., 55
Roth, G., 64
Roundtable technique (cooperative learning),
103
Routines (for student behavioral self-control),
52–53
Rules for adult-behavioral control management,
48–49

Scales, Pat, 95
Scenario determination (for resilience plan): for
academic efficacy, 30; for behavioral self-
control, 57; for caring/authentic relationships, 69; described, 9; for role of family,
96–97; for role of peer relationships, 83; for
self-selected learning goals, 42
School librarians: and academic efficacy, 23–29;
bullying intervention, 79–81; caring/
authentic relationships with student, 63–69;
goal setting for students, 38–41; learning
strategies for students, 26–29; peer support
training for students, 82; planning for resilience, 29–35, 41–45, 57–62, 69–74, 84–88;
role in peer tutoring, 107; student behavioral
self-control strategies, 47
Seifert, T. L., 26–27
Self-instruction (by students) learning strategies,
26–27
Self-modification strategies (for student behavioral self-control), 53–55; simplified, 55
Self-selected learning goals, 9, 37–45; evaluation
of work quality, 40; goal setting, 39; locat-
ing/identifying proper environment, 40;
observation/tracking task performance, 40;
planning for resilience, 42–45; school librarian role, 41; seeking help, 40–41; task analy-
sis/strategies, 39; time management, 39–40
Send-a-problem problem solving technique
(cooperative learning), 103

Sheldon, S. B., 65

Shure, M. B., 52

Standards for the 21-st Century Learner (American Association of School Librarians), 111–13

Students: academic efficacy strategies for, 23–29; adult-managed behavioral control of, 47–62; caring/authentic relationships with teachers, 63–75; desired behavior from teachers, 66; goal setting for, 38–39; planning for resilience of, 29–35; resilience in schools, 3–4; self-selected learning goals, 37–45; student-student persuasion, 24–25

Talking chips technique (cooperative learning), 103–4

Teachers: and academic efficacy, 23–26; behavioral control management strategies, 48–57; building student confidence by, 29; bullying intervention, 77, 79–81; caring/authentic relationships with students, 63–75; creating cooperative learning groups, 82; informal ongoing evaluations by, 7; interacting with families, 92; learning environment management, 29; Library Advisory Committee membership, 94; motivation statements used by, 27; observations inclusive of, 11, 17; parental contact by, 96; positive influences of, 4; teaching task management strategies, 39; ten commandments for, 67–69; use of ClassMap Survey by, 21

Ten commandments for teachers, 67–69

Thompson, J. J., 80

Three-step interview technique (cooperative learning), 104

Tokens (as rewards) for behavioral self-control, 50

United States resilience studies, 1–2

Vygotsky, L. S., 51–52

Walther, B., 47

West, R. P., 47

Wheler, P., 26–27

Young, K. R., 47, 55

Zimmerman, B. J., 37

About the Authors

CAROL A. DOLL is professor and graduate program director of the Library Science Program in the Department of Teaching and Learning at Old Dominion University, Norfolk, VA. She is the author of Collaboration and the School Library Media Specialist and coauthor of Bibliotherapy with Young People: Librarians and Mental Health Professionals Working Together.

BETH DOLL is professor and director of the School Psychology program at the University of Nebraska, Lincoln. NE. Dr. Doll is the author of Resilient Classrooms: Creating Healthy Environments for Learning and Transforming School Mental Health Services: Population-Based Approaches to Promoting the Competency and Wellness of Children, and the coauthor of Bibliotherapy with Young People: Librarians and Mental Health Professionals Working Together.